Convictions
of an Old Coach

Convictions
of an Old Coach

Joe North

The HiliHelen
Group Publishers LLC

Library of Congress

ISBN: 978-1-7361525-7-7

Printed and bound in the United States of America by Ingram Lightning Source

Front cover central art design by Rashad Davis with title and author name designed by Chuck Mays

Interior illustrations by Chuck Mays and Katie Gould

Editing, layout, and design by Jacque Hillman and Katie Gould

The HillHelen Group LLC
www.hillhelengrouppublishers.com
hillhelengroup@gmail.com

Table of Contents

Foreword

This book is about basketball. It is a collection of anecdotes from Joe North's coaching career: Some of them are about the art of the game, while others are reflections and life lessons from his childhood, growing up on a farm in Tennessee. In this book is the knowledge of a coach of more than forty years, for the benefit of athletes and his fellow coaches alike. His hope is that young coaches may garner some small benefit from his words so that he may continue coaching the next generation from the sidelines.

The following are testimonials from former players under Coach North.

In summer 1990, I was a rising junior at Adamsville High School in Adamsville, Tennessee, when our basketball team received the news we had a new coach. Not long afterward, we met Coach Joe North. Our first meeting was at the outdoor courts at the city park, where we played pickup games while Coach got his first look at his potential squad. Afterward, he shared his initial thoughts about our team's potential and the future of basketball at our school. I remember two things from that talk: First, this man immediately commands respect; and second, boy, I am glad he said that I was a good shooter.

Quickly, Coach North went to work changing the culture of the program—and there was work to be done. We had talent, especially for a 1A school, but we lacked a winning culture. That began to change once school began. First, we got in shape. We ran—a lot. We jumped—a lot. And we got stronger. A pull-up bar was installed in the gym. You couldn't go from practice to the locker room without doing your pull-ups, and it made a difference! I still brag about improving from managing one or two pull-ups to busting out twenty-five the next year. When the season began, practices were highly organized, with every minute of practice accounted for on a written practice plan. Coach demanded great effort every day, and there was an attention to detail that was new for us. We improved in our first season, highlighted by a home upset win against talented Bolivar Central, one of Joe's former schools. And we continued to improve the next year as the groundwork was laid for deep runs in the playoffs the subsequent years.

Coach's resume speaks for itself. He was successful with girls and boys, at small schools and large schools, with city schools and rural schools. I think several factors were responsible for his sustained success. First, Joe was a leader. He was in charge; he knew what he wanted to accomplish, and he had confidence in his ability to get the job done. Second, he had a deep understanding of the game of basketball from his years playing and coaching, as well as the time he put in learning the game from legends, such as Don Meyer from Lipscomb University. And third, Joe was a competitor.

I remember immediately being impressed with his toughness and no-nonsense approach to preparing to compete. His style was that of a parent—what some might call tough love. Players understood there would be consequences for their actions, but they also understood they had a supporter who would look out for them. I remember him saying on more than one occasion that his players were his children. As a player, you wanted to make Coach North proud *all* the time—not just when you were playing the game.

I consider myself fortunate to have played for Joe. I certainly became a better basketball player but, more importantly, he played a major role in my growth as a young adult. I remember one particularly honest talk that occurred during baseball

season. I wasn't playing very well at the time, and even though it wasn't basketball season, he was still my coach, and he made it a priority to give some timely coaching advice. Later, as I prepared to play college baseball, he suggested a book to read to help with the mental side of competing. More than any other coach I played for across my athletic career, Joe's focus was on developing people beyond players. He always took opportunities to talk about life lessons beyond basketball.

Undoubtedly, Coach had an influence on my career path, as I chose to become a teacher and coach. Nearly thirty years later, I apply lessons learned at Adamsville High School to my coaching now: organized practice plans, a focus on basic fundamentals (the shell drill is still the foundation for building defense), and talking about lessons bigger than basketball. Investing time in kids to build relationships, instilling discipline, and holding players accountable. These things worked then, and they work now. I am thankful to have had the opportunity to play for Coach Joe North and consider him both a friend and mentor.

—*Kevin Keen*
Science teacher, basketball and lacrosse coach
Asheville, North Carolina
Played for Coach North 1990–1992

Bolivar Central teams under Coach North played with a soundness at both ends of the floor that was seen in few teams in the area. They were always conscious of making it as difficult as possible for you to score. On the offensive end, they made it difficult for you to defend against them due to their ball-handling ability, movement, and patience in waiting for the right opportunity to score. From offensive positioning, footwork,

 shooting technique, and through every phase of defensive play to the final blockout when a shot is taken, Bolivar Central players always exhibited the results of Coach North's understanding of the game. There is no coach in Tennessee who did a better job of teaching his players how to play the game of basketball together than Coach North did during his time at Bolivar Central.

I have always told my players that the three key ingredients in success in basketball are playing hard, playing smart, and playing together (no man is an island). Just as Coach North was a great teacher of the skills of the game, he was also a great motivator of players in getting them to play to their potential. Coach North had an outstanding combination of teaching ability and motivational skill. I feel honored to have been asked to comment about this man who has given the game of basketball at Bolivar Central far more than he has taken away.

I can think of no better compliment that a basketball coach could ever receive than to be told by one of your teammates, "Mitch, you know your team plays a little bit like we used to play for Coach North at Bolivar Central."

—Stacy Ellis Mitchell
Head coach, girls basketball, Warren Central (Indianapolis,
Indiana) 2018 IHSAA Girls Basketball 4A State Champions
Played for Coach North 1982–1985

The first three words that come to mind when I think of Coach North are accountability, humor, and respect. Practice started at three o'clock sharp, and there were no exceptions. But I always remember we would start every practice with the plan for the day and a joke or a funny saying. He was all business, and there was going to be a purpose with every day, but that didn't mean that we couldn't laugh along the way. I

 admired how he always held us accountable for our actions on and off the court as well. We knew what was expected of us. His expectations held me to a higher standard, which is something I still remember now that I am out of sports and into my career. He demanded respect in how he coached, but he gave that respect back to his players. I never felt like I wasn't valued as a player, even though I was never the best on the court. I also knew his door was always open if I needed someone to talk to.

Among the many things that he taught me, I will always remember the most important thing is my faith. One of the last teaching moments he gave me as I left for college was "not to get too far to where I couldn't hear the church bells." Anytime I felt myself drifting from church, that's what I would remember. Coach North was my toughest coach throughout all my years of playing, but he's the one in only two years who taught me more life lessons than I could've asked for. I was lucky to have him the time that I did, wind sprints and all!

—Haley Elliott
Senior tax accountant, Ardent Health
Nashville, Tennessee
Played for Coach North 2009–2011

Going into my sophomore year (1995), Coach North had open-heart surgery. I can remember it like it was yesterday. He called me into his office and told me that he was suspending me for a year. He said that I needed to work on my attitude and figure out whether I truly loved the game of basketball. Granted, I will admit there were some things I needed to work on. He said that I would not understand this at the moment, but now, after getting older, I agree with him 100 percent. Coach North had a way of smoothing things over with me.

He informed me that they were bringing in a former coach. He also said I was a reason for him having surgery, and I needed not to make the new coach have surgery. He seemed so serious, but he chuckled after saying this.

The reason I am the person I am now is because of Coach North. The year off taught me valuable lessons that I try to instill in my players today. The selfless love, determination, and attitude adjustments are just some of the traits that stick out. I will never forget that day back in 1995 that changed my life. Thank you, Coach!

—*Preston Barbee*
Dyersburg High School, Class of 1998
Played for Coach North 1995–1998

 Coach Joe North taught me what it meant to believe in yourself. He was a genius at pulling out the gift in his players not only for basketball but for life itself. He is known to be one of the great innovators of our time on and off the court. There are not many coaches who are more kind, compassionate, fierce, and yet uncompromising in their approach to the game than Joe North. I will be forever grateful for what he pulled out of me.

—*Anthony Reed, Crockett County High School, 1988–1989*
Pastor of All Nations Christian Church (St. Louis, Missouri)
and school counselor for St. Louis City Public Schools
Played for Coach North 1988–1990

For one year, I got to play for Coach Joe North at Bells Eagles. It was in this setting that I came to understand the depth, compassion, competitiveness, and strength of this man. Coach was always committed to learning, teaching, and acting on his insights. That's why Coach was a winner wherever he went. I'm

 sure when you finish reading this book, you'll see that Joe North does not fit any stereotypes. He's a thinker, a compassionate man, a passionate man, and, most important, a leader from whom there is much to learn. I know I have.

—Tony Shutes
Head girls basketball coach at University School of Jackson
Jackson, Tennessee
Played for Coach North 1976–1977

"Girl, you've got GUTS!"

Whenever I think of Coach North, this quote comes to mind. My name is Danielle Barbee, and I played for Coach North at North Side High School in Jackson, Tennessee. He was a one-of-a-kind coach whom I still look up to. I consider him one of the best coaches ever. I credit him for helping me realize the guts and determination I had inside me. He challenged my teammates and me every single time we practiced and played a game.

Coach North introduced me to the common term of "conditioning" and the most feared daily "mile run." I remember it like it was yesterday. I was a freshman, and we were in the conditioning portion of the year before the official season. We ran and lifted weights on the football field every day during the hottest part of the day. Since Coach North set the expectation of performing your best and never giving up, I strived never to let him down.

One day, out on the field during the "mile run," I started wheezing. At the time, I didn't know I had asthma, so I kept running anyway. Coach North told me to stop, but I kept going because I didn't want to be considered a quitter or making excuses to quit. I still completed the mile. Once I was done, Coach North looked at me and said, "Girl, you've got some

 guts!" After that, he assured me that I shouldn't be stupid, and I needed to see a doctor about my wheezing during runs.

I enjoyed my entire experience and appreciated his ability to motivate and influence us to do what needed to be done. He always began each practice with a story or encouraging word to get us going. He also expected the best from us each and every time we stepped onto the court as well as in the classroom. His coaching and mentorship have played a huge role in shaping the person I am today.

I appreciate the fact that he still keeps up with me now that I'm grown, because finding educators and coaches who really care about you as a person and not just your performance is rare.

—*Danielle Barbee*
North Side High School, Class of 2005
Played for Coach North 1999–2003

So Why Coach?

Gandhi once said, "Nearly everything you do is of no importance, but it is important that you do it."

You coach because that is who you are. No one in the stands realizes or cares how many times you have mopped the gym floor. Most of the players don't. The truth is, the world will not stop if it is not perfectly cleaned, but you do it because there is something inside you that says, "All things matter." You do it for you—not in a selfish way, but in a fulfilling way.

I wonder: Can you not care about small things and still care about big things? If you don't take care of the small things, will there be as many big things?

You coach for the love of the game—the art of teaching individuals to work together and depend on each other to achieve their goals. You coach because you have a God-given gift to make a difference in the lives of others.

When someone calls me "coach," they pin a badge of honor on me. This badge should be worn with dignity and gratification.

"Nearly everything you do is of no importance, but it is important that you do it."
—Mahatma Gandhi

How to Be a Good Coach

1. Learn from the best.
2. Have the passion to be the best you can be.
3. Be willing to sacrifice time now for the future.
4. Be organized.
5. Be a good teacher.
6. Earn respect.
7. Be a good listener.
8. Lead by example.
9. Watch NBA and women's college basketball.
10. Don't sacrifice what is right now for wins.
11. Read everything written by John Wooden, Morgan Wootten, Dean Smith, Bobby Knight, Don Meyer, and others.
12. Find your niche.

1. Learn from the best.

As I started coaching in 1974, at age twenty-two, I was blessed to be the assistant coach to a great, motivating coach.

Mark Massey could get the most out of his players through encouragement, smiles, and body language. Coach Massey played at David Lipscomb University, and a new coach arrived there in 1974 who changed my life: Dr. Don Meyer was the smartest man I have ever met and the best coach I have ever seen.

Coach Massey was hired to work at Coach Meyer's summer basketball camp. I went along and asked Coach Meyer if I could work for free. He hired me for the next ten years. He was also a guest clinician at clinics that I held at my school many times. Coach Meyer was the master of paying attention to detail.

My high school coach was Marvin Williams. In the 1960s in West Tennessee, every team played zone. Coach Williams taught us the Army version of Bobby Knight's man defense, taking it a step further by playing full-court, deny-all-passes man defense. Coach Williams was also a great shooting instructor.

Because of Coach Meyer, I was able to work at many of Bobby Knight's camps and clinics. Coach Knight was a hard worker and demanded the best from everyone.

My favorite coach was Dean Smith. I met Coach Smith at a clinic and asked him if I could watch his practice, and he invited me to come. A week before our practice started, I traveled to Chapel Hill, fourteen hours away, and spent a week watching the University of North Carolina prepare for the season. His practices were extremely well organized and to the point. Coach Smith believed in "practice with a purpose."

Get mentored by great people. Learn as much as you can from them, and then apply what you have learned in your own style.

2. Have the passion to be the best you can be.
Passion means not only working to be the best but *wanting* to work to be the best. Passion must be a controlled desire, or

it can get away from you. It must be tempered with intelligence, patience, and perspective. Don't be that coach who is constantly yelling and never actually saying anything; let your players know you care by the way you prepare, teach, and observe—not by being just a loud cheerleader.

How do you get passion? First, you must love what you are doing. You must love to teach, and you must love the people you are teaching.

If you have average or less talent, you must have smaller victories. For this kind of team, you must have more of a loving passion. You must teach your players to be smart and connected; you must teach them to find a way to give themselves a chance in every game. For an above-average team, you must teach them never to be complacent. You must challenge them every day.

Passion will keep you going after heartbreaking losses. Passion will keep you young at heart. Passion will flow into other parts of your life. I cannot imagine life without passion.

3. Be willing to sacrifice time now for the future.

If you are a young coach and your friends want you to take trips, play golf, etc., when you could be working on your craft, you have to make sure you balance work and fun. If you sacrifice your job for fun without feeling guilty about it, you should re-evaluate yourself. This also applies to your family—put your family before fun or you will probably end up having *too much* time for fun in the end.

4. Be organized.

I suggest that you have daily basketball lesson plans, as well as daily classroom lesson plans. These plans should be based on weekly, preseason, first third, second third, and final third of the season (which is tournaments). I always planned my practice schedules based on the teams I must beat to get both to and past where I wanted to go.

I was once told, "If you come to practice once unprepared, you will know it. If you come to practice twice unprepared, the team will know it. And if you come to practice three times unprepared, all will know it."

5. Be a good teacher.

Most high school coaches make a lot more money for teaching than they do for coaching, yet they do not prepare very well for the classroom. You might have three to five classes with twenty to thirty-five students in each. Some of your students will be your players.

When you do poorly in the classroom, you are saying: "This class isn't important, and it doesn't matter."

"The only students at school who matter are my players."

"I really don't know what I'm doing."

"I don't care about learning, and neither should my players."

"I really don't appreciate how hard other teachers work."

"I'm a coach, and coaches aren't really teachers."

"It doesn't matter when my own kids hear students laugh about what a joke I am in the classroom."

I could go on and on about why some coaches don't think they should be a good teacher, but:

1. Earn your money.

2. Earn the respect of the students.

3. Earn the respect of other teachers.

4. Let your players know that you will not tolerate a poor classroom attitude.

5. It's the right thing to do.

6. It gives you self-respect.

John Wooden, Morgan Wootten, Woody Hayes, and Bobby Knight were all excellent classroom teachers.

6. Earn respect.

I find it interesting that, as a young coach, I thought I knew all of the answers. In reality, I didn't even know the questions. During my second year as a head coach, I received nine technical fouls. I wanted every call, and I was too quick to point out missed calls.

The best thing that happened to me was umpiring high school and college baseball and being on the other end. Most of the referees were very good at what they did and were not going to let a young, hotshot wannabe get by with anything without paying his dues. To my surprise, these same referees named me the Refs' Choice Coca-Cola Award Coach of the Year two years in a row before they discontinued it. I asked them why they picked me, of all people, for this award, and one of the refs told me the reason: They loved my passion; they loved how well my players behaved; and they hoped I would shut up if they gave me the award.

I learned that I had to earn their respect, and they were not going to give it to me without some work on my part.

As for earning coaches' respect, that's another matter.

Older coaches who did not work that hard resented me. Some coaches felt threatened by me, and others considered me a hotshot who was all show.

We had a lot of district games snowed out in a ten-team district, and seeding for the district tournament was next to impossible. I suggested a point system that I learned from Bill Emerson, a great former coach and leader in education in the state. The system was based on wins and losses versus teams with winning and losing records. All the coaches were trying to stay out of our bracket and Fayette-Ware's bracket. Fayette-Ware had Carlos Clark, who would later be SEC Player of the Year and a member of the Boston Celtics with Larry Bird.

I was cursed at and made fun of, but no one else had a

plan at all. Some wanted to draw names by chance for seeding. Finally, they agreed to my plan by a slim majority. Without exception, each coach who lost blamed me. I talked with one of my mentors, and he helped me through this difficult situation.

Eventually these coaches fell by the wayside, and I made sure, as I became a veteran coach, to help young coaches as much as I could.

7. Be a good listener.

There are many ways to be a good listener, but observation is one of the best. Stand in the hallway between classes and watch body language. Listen not only to words but also tone of voice and expression. When a student or player is upset, let them get it all out before you say anything. Ask your players what they think about a play or a team.

8. Lead by example.

I have a hard time with "Do as I say and not as I do." This goes for drinking, smoking, family, and teaching. Small things make a difference. For example: One week I mop the gym floor and pass the mop on to assistants, managers, and players, starting with seniors. This teaches that no one person is better than the others. Pick up trash in the halls. Go to other school functions such as plays, musicals, and soccer matches.

Take your team to functions as a group. This helps your players realize there are other worlds besides theirs. It also lets other students know you care about what they do.

9. Watch NBA and women's college basketball.

Good NBA teams are great pick setters and passers. Small college women's teams run great inbound plays and quick hitters. You won't get that much from big schools because it's more about athleticism than technique.

10. Don't sacrifice what is right now for wins.

One of my biggest mistakes was tolerating a bad attitude for a season. This player made the team and me miserable. I made a vow that I would never do that again. Do the math: 150 practices, thirty games. I would rather have fun 150 times than win one or two extra games out of thirty.

Bad attitudes create bad attitudes. They are usually caused by living the wrong way and doing the wrong things. You know what is right, and so do your players; if they don't, then teach them and demand that they live and do their best. Basketball without positive discipline is just playground entertainment.

11. Read everything written by John Wooden, Morgan Wootten, Dean Smith, Bobby Knight, Don Meyer, and others.

If you don't read their books, you are missing some marvelous insights on coaching and becoming a better person. Also, Meyer and Knight have some great teaching videos.

12. Find your niche.

Most people become unhappy because they advance at least one level above their happiness and God-given ability, whether it is middle school, high school, college, head coach, or assistant coach.

How do you know where your niche is? For me, the key was how well my players listened. I connected well at the high school level, but I feared this connection would not be there at the college level. I had many opportunities to become an administrator at various levels, but I selfishly stayed in coaching. My thought process was simple: I could make a lot more money as an administrator, but would my passion be there? Or I could make less money as a coach, but I would be doing what I loved.

Coach to your own personality. You can't be someone else. If you try to act like *your* coach, you will probably fail. You must be comfortable in your own skin to be happy. Some coaches can be successful as fear motivators. Some can be good at "cheerleading" their teams. Some coaches are more cerebral; others are analytical; others go by feel; and some have many of these traits. Whatever you're best at, make it the basis for how you coach.

True Grit

I read an article about common traits of successful people. It basically said that intelligence, looks, charisma, and talent are all important, but grit is what almost all successful people have in common.

I thought about this and looked at my life and the lives of my former players, coaches, and teachers, and I realized how on point this statement was.

What is grit? Wikipedia says that grit in psychology is a positive, non-cognitive trait based on an individual's passion for a particular long-term goal or end state, coupled with a powerful motivation to achieve their respective objective. Well, that's way too deep for a dumb coach to understand. To me, it means that when things get tough, you get tougher. It means that when you are running sprints and your side hurts, you suck it up and keep going. It means that when you and your wife are going through a tough time, you work through it because giving up is unacceptable. Grit means fighting through a tough season without making excuses and while getting everything you can out of your kids. Grit means doing the best with what you have and not worrying about what you don't have.

Can grit be taught? Absolutely.

People do not realize how much grit they have until they are put to the test.

Players must be challenged to bring out this toughness: They must be encouraged to be mentally and physically tough, but this should be done in the right way for the right reasons. One must not get grit and selfish stubbornness confused. Grit should be used to improve oneself and others, not the opposite.

I looked back at former players who displayed exceptional grit and realized how this helped them in other parts of their lives. As a coach, one of the most rewarding things is to realize that you had a small part in helping players realize their grittiness.

I learned grit from my father on the farm. He taught me how to keep working after I got tired. He taught me to get the job done, whether it was hauling hay, chopping cotton, or plowing. You keep going until it's done; quitting was never an option. Until I had developed grit to an acceptable level, he would monitor me. After I had developed grit in my work ethic, my father would trust me to complete my tasks on my own. Of all the lessons he taught me, grit was the one that carried me through the tough times so well.

I suggest you read *Grit* by Angela Duckworth; it is a good read for all coaches and players.

I Didn't Do It My Way

At a coaching clinic, I heard a successful coach sing every verse of Frank Sinatra's "I Did It My Way." As I listened to him sing and then give a speech on how he did it his way and how it brought him great success, I realized—and am so grateful—that my Savior didn't allow me to do things *my* way! If He had, I fear my life would be in total ruin right now.

I don't believe in luck per se, as others might. Sure, it is luck if you find a quarter on the sidewalk or a good parking spot opens. But the luck I'm talking about is success and happiness.

I don't believe it was luck that I got to play for one of the best coaches in the nation, Marvin Williams. Nor was it luck that I wasn't allowed to be his assistant out of college because of minority hiring at the time. Instead, I got to work under Mark Massey, who was the greatest motivator I have ever witnessed. It wasn't luck that through Coach Massey, I got to meet, work with, and be mentored by Dr. Don Meyer at Lipscomb University. Coach Meyer was the best I have ever seen at breaking things down and teaching the small details; his organizational skills were unmatched. It wasn't luck that Coach Marvin Day mentored me on how to handle tough situations and how to be a game coach: He was one of the best at controlling game tempo and using timeouts.

Nor was it luck the day I met my future wife, Nancy, for the first time. She became my best friend and my sounding board. She sat behind my bench and monitored the team. Nancy didn't know a lot about basketball at first, but she understood people. I learned, and am still learning, about people and personalities from her.

It wasn't luck that I can look back on my life and realize how blessed I have been. It was God's grace that allowed me to touch and be touched by other people's lives.

If I had done things my way, I would not have listened and learned from these marvelous people. If I had done it my way, there is no way my wife would have tolerated me all these years.

There is no one you can't learn from. Sometimes it might be what you shouldn't do, but still, this is learning. I suggest you watch games to pick up things someone does that might make you a better coach. Every coach does something better than you. During your planning period, observe a teacher who has it all together. You know you will pick up something you can use. You might even impress that teacher enough to support you and your team more.

Remember: Even Frank had his Rat Pack to mentor him.

Trust and Courage

I remember teaching my grandson to swim. He was four years old, standing on the pool edge, with me in the water. I had my arms out, encouraging him to jump to me, and I would catch him. I remember his face and all the fear in his eyes, and he looked into my eyes and jumped. He jumped because he trusted me more than he feared the water. This is a perfect example of courage.

I'm not sure you can ask your players to be courageous unless they trust in you. One of the biggest nights in my coaching life happened during a game against a major rival. We were losing by eight to ten points in the fourth quarter.

My wife, who always sat behind me, told Linc, our manager, "Coach had better do something or we're going to lose."

I heard Linc reply, "Don't worry, Momma. Coach always thinks of something."

I immediately called timeout and gave instructions, but for the first time, I looked deeply into the players' eyes and realized that they totally trusted me and would do exactly what I instructed them to do. We did win that game.

After every game, I always evaluated my coaching. But for the first time, I realized I really was a coach. Why? Because my players respected me because I gave them everything I had, every day in practice, and gave them every opportunity to be their best. I found that the secret to courage was, and is, trust. Without trust, there is not 100 percent commitment. Without commitment, the best-laid plans fail. *With* commitment, almost anything has a chance to work.

That night, I also reflected that I have to repay my players' trust in me by trusting them.

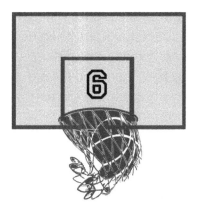

Rules to Live By

I don't do public speaking. I leave that to the professionals. But after I retired, the senior class of the school I retired from wanted me to speak at their senior graduation chapel. They were a special class, and I knew exactly what I would talk about.

When I was twenty-nine years old, the Good Lord grabbed me and made me realize what a miserable person I was. I had spent about ten years getting farther and farther away from God, but His love brought me back. It was then that I really got into the Bible.

I noticed that the Old Testament was a lot about rules and punishment, whereas the Gospels were more of a framework for making rules, much like our Constitution. The Gospels teach us that Jesus was about love, mercy, and grace. Jesus used stories, parables, and miracles, all based on love and faith, to reach one's soul. Jesus taught that one's cup should be clean on the inside, not only the outside, and if you have your heart right, you should be able to make your own rules as long as they are within God's parameters. Jesus wants to be your personal Savior, and I believe personal rules bring us closer to Him.

With this in mind, I would like to share some of my rules, sayings, and quotes based on God's word that I try to live by. Some are in my own words, some are borrowed, but nothing is new—just worded differently:

1. Love is an action word.

We say, "I love you," or "I love this and that," with a grain of salt, but do we really mean it? Like everything else, it is so easy to say and so hard to do.

My father never once said, "I love you" to me, but he showed his love for me every day: I remember playing American Legion baseball in Hattiesburg, Mississippi, and other faraway places, and there my mom and dad would pull up in their old pickup truck. They sacrificed to send me to college. They gave me everything I needed to make it through life. They lived love in everything they did. Yes, love is an action word.

2. Have great mentors.

Seek advice from people who can give great advice. They should care for you enough to want the best for you. I have had great mentors for my spiritual growth, finances, teaching, and coaching. My mentors were all older and wiser than I was, and most have moved on to be with Jesus. As I have learned from them, it is now my turn to mentor a few people; most are former students, players, and young coaches. It is a great honor to help others, and I do it with the greatest care and gratitude.

3. The wicked are blinded by their sins; they cannot understand why what they are doing is wrong.

We usually judge too quickly without thinking. This is a good way to build walls between you and others, destroying your chance to become a physical witness and to show God's love. Harping at people will only make the wall thicker and higher: Jesus used love and kindness to tear down walls.

4. Patience truly is a virtue.

God's plans for you will come if you have faith. Jesus spoke to my heart as clearly as if you had spoken to me and said, "I have something for you to do." I waited for Jesus to tell me what it was, but there was no answer. I started praying. I got to church thirty minutes early every time the door was open and sat there, reading the Bible and praying. Three months went by with no answer. Then, one Sunday, as clearly as the first time, God said, "Start a Fellowship of Christian Athletes chapter at your school."

I do not know exactly why God picked me to do this or why he wanted an FCA at this school at this time; I can only assume there was at least one person there who needed it.

I believe God had me waiting to prepare me for the job. That praying and reading the Bible did not hurt one bit. By the way, the FCA at that school grew to more than 100 members, and they did marvelous things while I was there and after I left.

5. Remember the mustard seed.

I have a sign on my back porch by the door that simply says "mustard seed." I end many of my prayers with these two words. Jesus asked us to have at least this much faith. A mustard seed is no bigger than the tip on a straight pin, but Middle Eastern mustard plants grow so large that birds nest in them.

6. God truly loves you, and Satan truly hates God, who loves you. So Satan must try to make your life worthless and miserable to get back at God.

I'm sure you have heard the Cherokee proverb about the little boy who asked his grandfather about life: The grandfather told the young boy about a terrible fight between two wolves that live inside us—one wolf is good, and the other is evil. The evil wolf is full of anger, envy, sorrow, regret, greed, arrogance, self-pity, guilt, resentment, inferiority, lies, false pride, superiority, and ego. The man told his grandson that the good wolf displayed joy, peace, love, hope, serenity, humility, kindness, benevolence, empathy, generosity, truth, compassion, and faith.

The grandson thought about it for a minute and then asked his grandfather, "Which wolf will win?"

The wise old Cherokee simply replied, "The one you will feed."

7. God has given you all the tools you need to defeat Satan and have a good life. All you have to do is figure out how to use them.

These tools include the Bible, prayer, talent, intellect, family, church, and mentors. The most important reason to go to school is to find out where your talents are. From there, you have to find the right education to enhance your talents. This education can be anything from college to hands-on training.

8. Do what is right, no matter what.

I guess the question is "What *is* right?" In John Steinbeck's epic novel, *The Grapes of Wrath*, as the Joad family is heading to California looking for work, they meet a man who lost his family to starvation. He tells the Joads that there is no hope in California. Someone asks Tom Joad if he thinks what the man said is true, and Tom says it was true *to him*.

So is being right objective or subjective? Many people believe totally different things and are willing to die for their beliefs. Let your conscience be your guide. Many people have risked everything because of their conscience: George Washington, Thomas Jefferson, Martin Luther King Jr., Alvin York, John Glenn, and others.

9. It is much easier to say 'no' and later say 'yes' than it is to say 'yes' and later say 'no.'

The best principal I ever worked for (and I worked for a lot of good principals) was Milton Basden. He was on top of everything and expected the coaches to be that way in the classroom and on the court. He almost always said no to coaches' requests for new uniforms and other gear. I finally figured out that he believed if you wanted and needed something badly enough, you would not only keep asking but you would have a detailed and convincing argument for why it was needed.

After he retired, the next principal was the opposite. The result was coaches buying things that were not necessary and putting the athletic program in peril. The principal had to learn to say no to things when he had already said yes. This caused great animosity between some coaches and him.

10. Never take people you love for granted. Go out of your way to let them know you appreciate them.

Mass media makes it easy to let people know you care, but nothing is as good as a handwritten letter or note. Everyone should read "The Magic of a Note" (you can find it online at www.coachmeyer.com).

Mother Teresa said, "When talking to someone, make them feel as if they are the most important person in the room."

I once read a story about a woman who went to the family lawyer and told him she wanted to divorce her husband. The lawyer was friends with them both and this would be difficult. He asked the woman why she wanted a divorce. She replied that the marriage was dead, and there was no romance.

The lawyer said he would represent her for free if she would do something for a month: She had to be exceedingly nice to her husband; she must dress up, cook his favorite meals, and so on. She agreed. So she dressed up for her husband.

When he came home, she greeted him at the door and had his favorite meal prepared and served by candlelight. After a few days, he called her from work and told her not to prepare dinner because he wanted to take her out.

The lawyer saw the woman about three months later and asked why she had not come back to see him. She replied, "Why, we have a great marriage and would never think of divorcing now."

Sometimes you have to make the first move. Whether you do or don't take your loved ones for granted, there is a good chance it will be reciprocated.

11. Disappointments are unavoidable, but discouragement is a choice.

We all have our disappointments. They can be small, like missing an answer to a test question, missing a game-winning shot, or being turned down for a job. Disappointment should be a motivator—it should be what fuels the next practice. Disappointments are usually fixable; if they are not, move on.

A main reason for practice during the season is to fix what the team is doing wrong. Disappointments turn into discouragement when you don't fix what is wrong.

When players see that you are energetically fixing problems, they will become encouraged; they will buy in and become united with you and each other.

12. Be what you is, not what you ain't, 'cause if'n you ain't what you is, then you is what you ain't.

In 1978, I had the privilege of working a basketball camp with Wes Unseld, an NCAA All-American at Louisville. He played for the Washington Bullets from 1968 to 1981. He was the second pick in the NBA Draft, NBA MVP in 1969, Rookie of the Year in 1969, and inducted into the NCAA Hall of Fame in 2006.

Wes brought his father with him to the camp. Wes Senior told the kids the above quote; he was uneducated but wise. If you analyze this statement, it basically means: Don't live a lie. Actions speak louder than words, and don't call yourself a good person but do bad things.

A good test for your team is to have each player rank the others on the team and themselves from one to ten on character issues such as honesty, work ethic—anything you want on the chart. Then compare how the players view themselves to how others view them. Never let them know the results. This could give you a starting point to see how you can mold your kids into better people and players.

13. If you always do what you always did, you will always get what you always got.

You should not do things the same way and expect different results. It amazes me to watch kids in study hall preparing for a test: They go over everything in their notes instead of only going over what they don't know.

I had a player who was tall but shot the ball from the middle of his chest. I raised his shot and explained to him that he was wasting his height by shooting the ball from such a low release point. After reminding him several times about his release point, we had a "come to Jesus" meeting, and after that he changed his shot. He later became an All-State player and a Small College All-American, and played professionally in Europe.

This rule applies to coaches as much as it applies to players. I was a young coach with a talented team. Like most young coaches, I was running every drill I learned while I was playing. We were running the figure eight (grapevine) drill, and one of my players, Ricky Griggs, now a West Tennessee district attorney, asked me why we were running the drill. I answered, "Because it helps work on the fast break." I went home and thought about the drill. I realized that we never passed the ball and weaved behind the receiver in a game. I never ran this drill again, but I developed a transition drill based on our fast-break principles that was much more effective.

Bill Walsh was the coach of the San Francisco 49ers in the 1980s. After winning the Super Bowl and the next year missing the playoffs, Coach Walsh analyzed every play the team ran for the entire season and realized that they ran more than thirty plays that never worked. He took those plays out of the playbook. The result was that the 49ers were Super Bowl champions again.

You can't practice, study, treat people, listen, read—anything—the same way if you want to get better. Don't be afraid to learn new ways of doing things. One of the best books I ever read was *If It Ain't Broke . . . Break It!* by Robert J. Kriegel and Louis Palter; it explains this concept well.

14. HALT.

Don't make decisions when you are too:
- Hungry
- Angry
- Lonely
- Tired

I stole this anagram from Dr. Charles Stanley, and I love it.

Hungry: I don't know about you, but I should never go to the grocery store when I'm hungry. Remember, Esau gave up his birthright for a bowl of soup. Hunger can cause panic, anxiety, and anger.

Angry: Have you ever said something out of anger that you wish you could take back? I have learned through my mistakes to walk away when I am angry. At home, I clean the house, wash dishes, or mow the yard until I have coped with my anger. I guess you could say that I work it off.

Some people believe that anger is always bad. Anger can cause you to right an injustice; it can cause adrenaline to increase and give you the energy to overcome. If used the right way, it can be great. Sometimes I write on my practice schedule, "Get mad." I might slam the ball down or say those magic words: "Line up." If I am mad, I immediately go to an easy drill until I cool off. I never confront a referee when I am angry. I learned the hard way that I will see them again down the road. When the game is over, it's over. Move on.

Lonely: Sometimes I think loneliness is a selfish emotion. There is an old saying: "If you don't think about yourself, you will never be unhappy." We only want people to like what we like and to do what we do. If our friends are not in our world, we become lonely.

My wife married a coach. She had to give up a big part of her life to become part of mine. She has had to listen to my many problems with my team and school. I began to realize how much she had invested in me, and I, selfishly, was not investing in things important to her. I knew she loved antiques, so we started buying and selling antiques as a second job. She's happy that I loved her enough to give up such activities as softball and golf to do things with her, and I am happy to have my best friend at my side; it's a win-win.

Tired: Do you wait till the last minute to get things done and then work to exhaustion doing them? You probably got tired and were sloppy as you got closer to the end.

I think it was Vince Lombardi who said, "Fatigue makes cowards of us all."

I made my high school basketball team as a freshman because other players couldn't take the work, and they quit. I remember the last day of tryouts: Another player with a lot more ability than I had would always slow down when he got tired; he made me look a lot faster than I was. I got the last uniform. I wonder what would have happened to my life had I not made the team. I know what happened to the other player's life, and it was sad.

When tired, you tend to see the worst in things and become frustrated. If a player quits the team, I give him twenty-four hours to change his mind because the move is usually made out of frustration, and I want him to sleep on it to make a rested decision.

15. You are your family's legacy.

People have probably made great sacrifices for you to succeed. It was likely your parents, but this support could go much further back than that.

My father broke a chain of drunkenness, abusiveness, and ignorance. I owe so much to him. I am his legacy. Every good thing I do is partly because of him and my mother, and in some sort of way, it is for him. My kids and grandson are my legacy: It is my job to teach them to be the best they can be.

16. A kind word turns away wrath.

There is no defense for a kind word. I love the TV commercial called "Pass It On."

At my second school as head coach, I replaced my high school coach. He was at a different school than when he coached me and had just taken a college job. I got his job mainly because of his recommendation. He was a legend and probably the best coach in the state at that time.

The lady passing out food in the cafeteria line loved the old coach, so she thought she had to hate me. If we had chicken, she would dig around until she could find the worst piece and put it on my plate, then stare me down.

I thought about this and decided to use kindness instead of retaliation: No matter what my tray of food looked like, I smiled, thanked her, and told her to have a blessed day. By Thanksgiving, I could not eat all the food she would put on my tray. We became friends for the next ten years, until I left.

17. Be sincere.

Webster describes sincerity as being genuine and not being deceitful. I am convinced that you have to learn sincerity: You have to buy in and focus on the object of your sincerity. Human nature causes our minds to wander and express opinions without giving complete understanding to what is being done or said. In basketball, you must learn to totally commit to the team; to work for selfish reasons is deceitful and will only hurt the team. Sincerity means locking in at practice and not only going through the motions.

There are many great examples of people who always did their best. I can think of no one who personifies this more than Pete Rose; he is the all-time Major League Baseball hits leader; he never gave up on an at-bat, no matter what the score. He came to the majors as a second baseman, and he hit. He moved to left field, and he hit. He went from there to third base, and he hit. He finished his career at first base, and he hit. He led two teams to world championships and never took anything for granted. What he did as a manager had nothing to do with his sincere approach as a player.

18. Anytime you are full of yourself, hurting, prideful, lonely, have been wronged, or just have that weird feeling inside . . .

Read 1 Corinthians chapter 13.

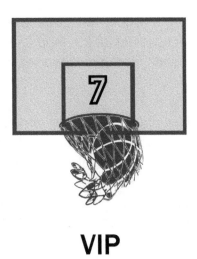

VIP

VIP stands for vision, initiative, and perspective.

Vision

Vision means that you must be the star of your own movie. You must visualize yourself and what you will be doing five, ten, and fifteen years from now.

For example, if you plan to be a surgeon, you should visualize yourself performing surgery. You should also see yourself carrying out the day-to-day operations of a doctor.

Initiative

Initiative means that you must do what it takes to accomplish your vision for yourself.

For example, if you are a high school student, you should take the classes necessary to accomplish your vision. Shadow people already doing what you plan to do someday. When you focus on your vision, it will help keep you on track.

Perspective

Perspective means you must understand that plans do not always work out exactly the way you expect. Life can get in the way—such events as marriage, death, and injuries. The difference between people who live their vision and those who do not is often how they handle disappointments and setbacks.

Another important point is the vision you see for yourself should be within your God-given talents. If you are not talented in a certain area, you probably should not make that your vision.

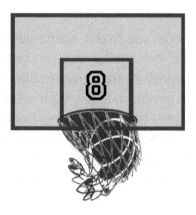

Mind the Gap

If you go to London and ride the subway, you will see a sign that says "mind the gap." It refers to the space between the ramp and the step of the train. You don't want to get your foot caught in that space!

This is true with coach-player relationships. One of the traps a young coach can fall into is to become buddies with players on his team. If you do this, you will always have problems with players and parents. You will lose respect as a coach. Why should a player respect a coach who is "just one of the guys"?

I'm not saying you should not care about your players. I'm saying you should not be one of them. My best advice is to keep a gap between you and them—one that is not so wide they cannot hear you or you cannot hear them, but the gap should be wide enough that the players are not jumping to your side and helping you make decisions, nor are you jumping to their side to be one of them.

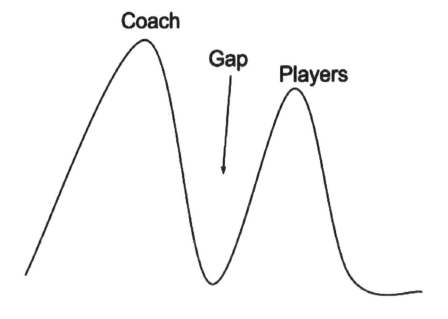

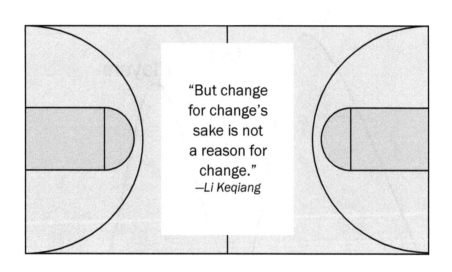

"But change for change's sake is not a reason for change."
—*Li Keqiang*

If It Ain't Broke . . . Break It!

Everyone should read this book by Robert J. Kriegel and Louis Palter. Published in 1991, *If It Ain't Broke . . . Break It!* basically says that if you stay the same, your competition will catch and surpass you.

Influenced by Bobby Knight and his rules and strategies, coaches in the 1960s and 1970s had to adapt because of the three-point line and changing officiating. The coaches who refused to change were passed by those who made the adjustments. In the 1980s and 1990s, most coaches were influenced by Dean Smith and his four-corner offense. The shot clock ended the four-corner offense. From the 1990s until 2010, Coach Mike Krzyzewski's style of taking outstanding players and developing their team skills for four years dominated. From around 2010 until recently, Kentucky, Kansas, and, later, Duke recruited the one-and-done players with great success. Recently, the trend of a combination of four-year players mixed with foreign players has proven successful. Teams such as

Villanova and Gonzaga have done very well with this strategy.

What happens to coaches who don't adjust? On the high school level, they fall into mediocrity. In major colleges, they get fired or retire. Coach Bobby Knight was fired at Indiana; he went to Texas Tech and left after mediocre seasons, and his son was fired shortly after replacing him. Gene Keady went by the wayside at Purdue as did many coaches at schools such as Vanderbilt and Northwestern.

Other coaches adapted to the new style of "entertainment basketball" and the star players of the one-and-done system. Coach K, John Calipari, Jim Boeheim, and Bill Self all adapted.

My high school coach was way ahead of everyone in the 1960s and 1970s, but by the 1980s, many good coaches had caught up to him. He had a great run, but he found it hard to change what had worked so well for so long. His full-court, deny-everything defense was his main offense. His offensive sets were based on getting the ball inside to the big man. It was hard to accept taking a 35 percent three-point shot when you could get a 55 percent post shot. John Thompson at Georgetown had a hard time with this as well.

I don't think these coaches are wrong, but I do believe the way the game is officiated and new rules have forced changes for the sake of entertainment over discipline and teamwork.

With new changes in the rules, coaches must find new ways to progress and improve. One must remember that most basic fundamentals never change and should be instilled through daily practice. One example is the charge call. In the 1980s, we had a team goal of five charges every game, and we ran if we didn't accomplish it.

Players received a milkshake for each charge taken. By the 1990s, referees in our area refused to call the charge; it was either a block or a no-call, so I quit putting an emphasis on the charge because it hurt us more than it helped us. We worked on the help defender blocking the shot instead. The charge came back a few years later, and taking the charge came back into play. Now, with the Eurostep, it is almost impossible to take a charge.

I personally like change. Change keeps your mind young. It forces you to get creative; it connects you with the younger generation. Not everything young people do or listen to is bad, and if it is bad, shouldn't you know what it is so that you can guide them to find a better way?

When I was young, I didn't trust older people because they were cynical. After I got older, I realized that cynicism is not age-related—it is heart-related.

With that being said, a lot of old things have lasted through the test of time, and we must have doors of communication open to pass them on.

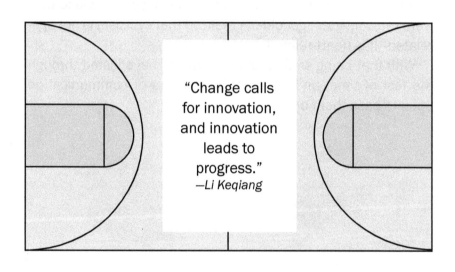

"Change calls
for innovation,
and innovation
leads to
progress."
—*Li Keqiang*

Criticism

There are two kinds of criticism: Constructive and destructive. Sometimes, they run into each other. Since this does happen, you must evaluate them both—you must go outside yourself and listen to the words and not the intent to have a true evaluation. Be thick-skinned but not blindly stubborn. Don't let a tone of voice keep you from hearing what someone has to say. Tell the person you will look into it; never tell them they are wrong or right until you have objectively analyzed the information. Trust yourself to make the right decision. After all, you want what is best for the team. No coach likes losing, but which is more important—your pride or the team?

Robert Lee or Kenneth? Robert was a five-foot-seven-inch point guard who played behind a great point guard until his senior year. Robert was not a good shooter, but he played hard and made good decisions. He was great at putting the ball in the shooters' hands at the exact time to shoot.

Kenneth was a talented sophomore. He was quick, long, and

smooth. My basketball cronies at breakfast every morning told me I was crazy for playing Robert over Ken. They were not at practice every day and did not know Robert's heart. They did not see how fluid the team was with Robert in charge.

In the regional semifinals, we were losing by 12 points with 2:24 left to play. Robert refused to lose and was directly involved in a 12–0 run that took us into overtime. We won the game. Then we won the regional tournament and lost in six overtimes to the No. 1 team in the state. Robert fouling out in that game was a real blow. Robert had intangibles and heart that Kenneth was still developing. Kenneth went on to become a great player for me. I think playing under Robert helped him a lot.

Bacon and Basketball

Bacon always gets your attention. I'm referring to Francis Bacon, considered to be the father of the scientific method. I have used the scientific method many times to solve a basketball problem.

The steps of the scientific method are:
1. State the question.
2. Collect information.
3. Form a hypothesis.
4. Test the hypothesis.
5. Observe.
6. Record and study data.
7. Draw conclusions.

An example of a time I used the scientific method was with a team I coached in the 1987–1988 season. The players were good shooters, but their overall free-throw percentage was hovering around 68 percent and was barely above 50 percent in the fourth quarter.

1. My question was: "How can we improve our free-throw percentage to around the 75 percent mark, especially in the fourth quarter?"

2. I started collecting information. I broke down shooting by quarters and by players.

3. My hypothesis was this: If we shoot more free throws in practice, under more stress and conditioning, then we will increase our free-throw percentage to at least the 75 percent mark in all quarters.

4. To test the hypothesis, we did the following:

   a. We started shooting free throws after every hard drill.

   b. Drills were created that gave rewards and punishments (usually running) for makes and misses. These drills included:

   - One-and-one after every drill by players from three different positions—point guards, two and three positions, and four and five positions
   - One-handed free throws
   - Free throws and sprints in groups of five; the goal is to make fifteen in a row (for example, if seven are made in a row and a player misses, his group runs eight sprints)
   - Line free throws—the team lines up in two groups at each end, and each player in the group shoots a one-and-one; if a player misses the first, his group runs two sprints; if he makes the first and misses the second, the group runs one sprint
   - Free-throw gotcha
   - Rapid-fire free throws

5. I observed that most players recognized the emphasis placed on free-throw shooting and worked harder before, during, and after practice on their own. Fatigue became less of a factor. Players were more engaged because every time a free throw was missed, players ran.

6. I recorded the following data: Free-throw percentage increased for every player except one player who was already meeting high standards. The team free-throw percentage was at 81 percent the rest of the season. The fourth-quarter free-throw percentage rose to 78 percent.

7. My conclusion was that players were not practicing free throws with the effort and accountability necessary to be prepared for the pressure of a game. Once pressure was put on the players during practice, they were more prepared for game pressure. Being in great physical shape didn't hurt, either.

Always have a reason for what you do.

Choosing a Team

Win-win

If your team is successful, everyone who has some ability—and a few who do not—will try out for the team. I have had as many as seventy people try out for my team.

There are many ways to pick a team. I encourage you to go to teachers, counselors, and administrators to check out the kids whom you don't know much about and are strongly considering. The best source of information might come from your best players and your manager. Never ask borderline players because they might consider a new player a threat to their playing time.

I tried to keep one player who had a lot of talent but had a bad attitude. If he loved basketball enough to straighten out, it was a win. If he did not, I would throw him off the team when the best opportunity came. This helped the team understand that there were consequences to a bad attitude.

You must love basketball more than you love being stupid.

Why I don't cut seniors

If a kid who makes the team as a freshman has tolerated me and all the work and time spent, he deserves to be on the team. You cannot ask your player to be loyal to you if you are not loyal to him.

If you have a senior on the team who doesn't get a lot of playing time, you must develop a special relationship with him. Try to appeal to his qualities such as leadership and work ethic. You should recognize his intangible characteristics every chance you get.

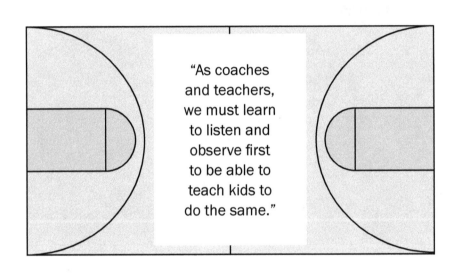

"As coaches
and teachers,
we must learn
to listen and
observe first
to be able to
teach kids to
do the same."

We Hear, But We Do Not Listen

My grandson, Hunter, has severe dyslexia. He basically sees everything three-dimensionally. Words on a page are flat and one-dimensional; therefore, when he looks at a page, the words are jumping up at him and moving. He thought this was normal, so he did not know how to explain his reading difficulties. He struggled in school. Kids can be so cruel. They told him he was dumb and made fun of him. Even though he struggled with reading, he could look at the pictures and usually comprehend the story.

I did not know what the problem was until I was taking him home one day, and as we were going down the road, Hunter said, "Look at the deer." There was a field about 100 yards long with a patch of woods behind it. I stopped my car to look and could see nothing. Then a deer walked out of the woods. I realized then that Hunter saw things differently.

I sent him to Will Beyer, clinical psychiatrist for the Jackson-Madison County School System, who set up an appointment to have Hunter tested at Middle Tennessee State University. We found out about his dyslexia and how to work around it. Hunter was put in a special program at the private school he attended.

At the end of the third grade, the headmaster told Hunter's mom that Hunter was not college material, and they did not want him back. Hunter was crushed. His self-esteem was broken. His mom quit her job to homeschool him, and I put him in taekwondo classes. Master Choi was fantastic with him. When we went somewhere to eat, I had him order and pay for the food. He became tougher, and his overall observation skills compensated for his struggle with reading.

One of our favorite things to do was go to the mall, observe strangers, and make up stories about them. In these stories, the shoppers ranged from being CEOs to sociopaths.

I told Hunter many times that the trials he was going through were preparing him for something unbelievable in his future. At age fourteen, he discovered music, and since then, he has written more than 200 songs about such topics as bullies, the so-called "cool kids," schizophrenia, imaginary girlfriends, invisible people, date rape, suicide, evil, revenge, and—of course—love. He has learned to be a deep thinker and has a special attraction to the uncool kids. His band, The Skeleton Krew, has done very well and has a lot of music on social media and videos on YouTube. I wonder what would have happened if not for that deer in the woods.

Listening and seeing go hand in hand. I have learned that you must look into people's eyes and through their eyes when you talk to them. Talk to kids about things they like. After they get started, just shut up and listen. Watch their body language and expressions, and listen to their tone.

Try to teach kids to know themselves and not be afraid to ask questions. When you disagree with them about a subject, let them talk it out and find a common ground to express your point of view. Ask them about cause, effect, and the big picture. Let them get their own results, not the ones that you have planned for them.

As coaches and teachers, we must learn to listen and observe first to be able to teach kids to do the same.

Dealing With Parents

I only have two rules when dealing with parents.

Rule No. 1: Don't argue with parents.

Remember: Parents have their own child in mind and not the team. They will literally keep track of the times their children start, the minutes they play, and what you say to them when you take them out as compared to what you say to other players. Parents will compare playing time with other players, awards given, words said in the newspaper and on the radio—you get the idea.

Parents will watch when you talk to other parents. Remember: Most parents are going to compare you to Coach K and not other high school coaches.

Parents will attack you at strategic times. If you win a big game but their kid was not an integral part, you will be attacked to steal the joy. If you lose a big game and their kid did not play well, it must be your fault, and they will let you know.

If a parent was not your friend before their child played, keep it that way until the child can't play for you anymore. Remember: Do things that earn respect. If parents don't appreciate this, then just move on. When parents want to talk to you, do not argue with them. You are never right in their eyes, and they will use everything you say against you.

I only had two parent meetings. One was my first year as a head coach at a small school. I was the high school boys' coach, freshman boys' coach, and high school baseball coach. It was a great school with a great leader in Bill Emerson.

Our freshman team went undefeated during the season, and in the county championship, we played a team we had barely beaten during the season in their own gym, and we lost by one point. We were so disappointed. The next day, the parents of my sixth man met with me. They unloaded on me because their son was not a starter and a star on the team. I argued with them as I explained that he was lazy and did not deserve to start. We all left exhausted and angry. I talked to Mr. Emerson about what had happened, and he explained that I should not fight battles I could not win. Lesson learned.

Bench conduct is important to me. My wife would always sit behind the team during games and report to me on the bench decorum. When a player came out of the game, he had to touch hands with every coach, player, and manager before he sat down. He also had to communicate with the player going in for him, explaining who he was guarding.

I had a player who made the team only because he played so hard. He was an okay, small athlete with little skill, but his father thought he was the best player on the team. He worked his way up to be the seventh player, second off the bench. During a game in which he played a lot of minutes, I took him out, and he touched everyone's hand until he got to mine. When he got to mine, he intentionally pulled his hand away. I said nothing. The next game, I did not play him at all.

After this game, his father trapped me in my office. He spent thirty minutes telling me what a great player his son was when he played and how bad a coach I was and how ridiculous it was for me not to play his son simply because he disrespected me. I said nothing. After the man finally stopped talking, I asked him if he had anything else to say.

He looked stunned and said, "I guess not. Don't you have anything to say?"

I said, "No. Have a good night." Then I walked out of my office and left him there.

I never had another problem with him or his son, or anyone else on the team. If you are right, you don't have to defend yourself. If you argue, you are only trying to win a battle of words with an angry parent. Just don't go there.

Rule No. 2: Make it clear that the team is a hierarchy, and you, as the head coach, are at the top.

If a parent calls because he believes his kid deserves more playing time, that kid does not play the next game. The result will be no such phone calls.

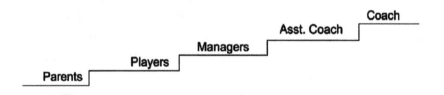

You should beware of such things as Christmas parties organized by parents. You should also beware of favors. I have been offered a new car to put a kid on the team. Remember, all parents want the most for their kids. Sometimes, they get "most" and "what's right" mixed up.

I fear that I sound cynical, but I truly believe it is best to separate yourself from parents until all is done. I use the word "attack" when I talk about parents because that is exactly what an interaction with them can be. It can be an attack on your character, coaching, and decision-making ability. Coaching comes with varied experiences and sometimes tough decisions.

"Players will
be loyal when
they think
you are."

Connections

Coaches will *tell* you they care about their players, but their *actions* tell the story. Let your players know that they are important and that basketball is important, but at the same time, hold yourself and your players accountable for their actions. The following are things I did at Bolivar Central and other places I coached.

When the whistle blew, there would be no more shots, and my players had to get into triple threat position. If a player shot the ball after the whistle blew and it went in, there would be no punishment, but if he missed, he owed me ten sprints or one lick with a paddle.

Devon Lane had to shoot a three-pointer after the whistle at the end of every practice. Needless to say, he became a great clutch shooter.

I bought an old van and took my players to Ole Miss, Union University, Freed-Hardeman University, and other schools to watch college games. I made sure my players had good nutrition.

I took every player capable of playing college basketball on visits to college campuses.

Each player had to not only pass their classes but make at least an eighty in every subject, every grade, period. For each point below eighty, they had to run ten suicide sprints or take one lick with a paddle. Eighty is average. I don't want my players to accept average in anything.

School morality is based on the attitudes of the most popular students; the athletes are usually part of this group. If the athletes have a good attitude in the classroom, it will affect the entire school. Players will learn how to study and be accountable. Thus, when they get to college, they are more prepared. Thirty-one players during my ten years at Bolivar Central played college basketball on some level. Twenty-nine of them graduated from college.

Each day, take home a different player who does not have transportation. Stop and buy them a snack on the way. Set up an account at a Quick Mart that only you can use as a part of your budget. Players will be loyal when they think you care.

Game Speed

On the first day of practice every season, I always run the same teaching drill. This drill benefits all of the newcomers to the team.

1. I leave a ball on the far end of the court.

2. I blow the whistle and tell all of the players to line up on the end line.

3. I ask one of the newcomers to run to the other end, get the ball, and bring it back to me.

4. I time the player's trip, which is usually approximately fifteen seconds.

5. I pull a $100 bill out of my wallet and toss it on the ground, then toss the ball to the end of the court.

6. I then tell the same player that if he can make the trip in less than ten seconds, he can have the $100 bill.

7. He will sprint as hard as he can, but since I have the clock, he will not make it.

8. I then ask if anyone else would like to try, and most of the

newcomers will try. But since I have the clock and whistle, all will come up just short.

The point of this exercise is this: The first trip was at the player's own speed, and the others were at game speed. Money motivated game speed, and money should be replaced by passion and exceeded by a desire to be the best. You cannot get better unless you go outside your comfort zone.

Team Rules

Lee Trevino said that the rules of golf should be no more than could be written on a matchbook cover. The more rules you have, the more you will end up breaking. I have two major rules that are similar:

1. Act right or I will deal with you.

2. You've got to love basketball more than you love being stupid.

Elvis and Carlton got into a fight in practice. I made both run 100 timed sprints. Elvis was six feet three inches tall and weighed about 160 pounds. Carlton was about six feet tall, weighed about 200 pounds, and had thick legs. Elvis made it through the punishment okay, but Carlton's legs locked up on him, and he was injured from the running. So was the punishment the same? I do not think so. You must evaluate everything when it comes to rules and discipline.

I believe rules for seniors should be much tougher than for freshmen. I believe in second chances, not so much in third chances. I found out that two freshmen were at a party using marijuana and drinking beer. I got them to come clean about the incident. Over a two-week period after practice, they and I then watched eighteen hours of videos on the effects of drugs and alcohol on the human body. They had to write a paper each night on the video and do some running.

As a junior, one of those two was seen drinking, along with another player. The question was: How do I handle a first-time and a second-time offender? The issue was this: They were juniors; one had already been disciplined, and the other was a first-timer. I suspended both of them for two weeks. The first-time offender had to run 100 sprints during practice, watch videos, and write papers on them for five days. The second-time offender had to run 100 sprints for ten days. Both had to dress in the PE dressing room until they re-earned the right to dress in the basketball dressing room.

The first-time offender never got into trouble again. The second-time offender got into trouble his senior year and was dismissed from the team. Did I do this right? How can you tell? Two of the kids never got into trouble again, and one is a successful coach today.

You Never Know

A few days before writing this, I was at an auto garage when a young man around thirty years old or so came up to me and asked me if I was Coach Joe North. I looked at him and recognized his face. I asked him if I owed him any money, and he said no.

I said, "Then yes, I am Coach North."

The young man asked whether I remembered him, and I told him that I remembered him from a history class. He said that he had wanted to talk to me for a long time and to thank me.

He went on to remind me of a conversation we had about his speech impediment and how I told him that it would make him stronger if he would develop his other talents to the best of his ability. I told him to never be like those who tried to tear him down.

He said he went home that day, thought about what his talents were, and realized he loved to cook.

Long story short, the young man went from being a cook to a

chef, to owning his own restaurant, to selling it for a large profit, and now owning three nice restaurants and still cooking in one of them.

All I did was encourage a discouraged young man. Every so often, a kind word and advice do make a difference.

Hang Around Good People

One of my pet peeves is when people fail to learn from those who went through what they are going through and came out on top. Young people call and send letters asking me to invest money that I don't have in their investment company. I always ask them how much they have invested, and that usually ends the conversation.

As a young coach, I worked coaching camps and clinics to listen and learn from successful veteran coaches more than I went to teach the kids. I remember sitting in dorm rooms talking about basketball situations until two or three in the morning and then waking up at six o'clock to work the camp.

I remember asking the best teachers how they handled situations. I remember sitting in their classrooms during my planning period to watch them teach. Some of the best advice I ever got came from these people, and I felt myself drawn to them.

I wonder how much more kids at church could learn from a

wiser youth leader than from one who is barely older than they are and who is trying to dress and talk like a teenager in order to fit in. These youth leaders believe this will cause them to be liked so they will be able to reach the kids.

I fear that today, most people consider older people to be out of touch with the world, when in reality, they see the world as it is. I know that age itself doesn't make you wise, but if you have the ability to be wise, I would think life experience might help.

The Magic of a Note

After retiring for a couple of years, I decided that I should substitute teach. I missed the interaction with the kids, and I thought I could pick and choose the days I wanted to be there (but that's another story).

The school principal, Don Roe, was an intelligent and diligent person. A few days after I subbed, I got a note in the mail from him thanking me for doing a good job. It made me feel good that someone cared enough to do this. Then I remembered a handout titled "The Magic of a Note." Everyone should Google and read this short story.

Taking the time to write a note of appreciation and mail it is so rare these days.

It says that, in some way, someone is special; it places value on a "thank you" and takes it to a higher level. It will put a bounce in your step and a smile on your face.

Why write a thank-you note? When you write, your mind expands, and how you feel flows out of the ink and onto the paper. It is personal and touching. It makes you human and vulnerable. Basically, the best of you comes out.

I suggest you write your wife, husband, child, or parents a note. Thank them for what they mean to you. Thank them for the little unnoticed things they do for you. Let them know that they have made a difference.

All I can say is, would a note like this mean something to you? I have obtained several of these notes. One is framed. Another is in my Bible. And all are saved in a special place.

Giving Advice

Basically, my purpose in writing this book is to give advice based on the many mistakes I have made. If you do not like to read about others' opinions and advice, you probably stopped reading before you got here anyway. One thing I have learned about advice is that it is easy to give and hard to take. When I gave my kids, players, and students advice, my only hope was that, if it was useful, they might remember and use it someday.

I have learned throughout the years that giving advice, suggestions, or recommendations without being asked is not appreciated and is sometimes insulting to the person you are advising. Sometimes people will take it as butting in, as demeaning; so I try not to give advice or opinions unless I am asked for them. At the same time, people should constantly seek opinions and advice from those they respect and those who have already experienced what they are going through.

At a school where I was teaching and coaching, the administration debated installing an expensive security system.

The school was large and spread out. I overheard them talking about the potential of this security system, but I was concerned that teachers and others working late would set off the alarm. I suggested that they not put the system in and instead hire janitors to do the heavy cleaning from 10 p.m. to 6 a.m. while no one else was there. Since workers and custodians would be there, an expensive security system would not be necessary.

The administration was amused by my suggestion but went ahead and put in an expensive system. They paid quite a lot for monitoring and upkeep. As I expected, it was set off so many times that they seldom turned it on. Because of the expense, they could not afford to hire the needed workers.

Because of this debacle, I have learned that a good way to give advice is to make it the other person's idea. Drop thoughts into the person's head and hope they can formulate those thoughts into concepts themselves. It doesn't matter who gets the credit for anything as long as it gets done and benefits come from it.

You Do Not Have to Agree With Someone to Love Them

The mentality that if you and I disagree, then we must hate each other bothers me. I fear this has become an epidemic, especially with the advent of social media. I follow Facebook mainly to keep up with what my grandson is doing in his quest to be a rock star. It troubles me that such harsh words are used that polarize people into specific groups.

People have a lifetime to figure out life. Along the way, many mistakes will be made. Some of these mistakes will be careless, others honest, and some intentional (though these are called decisions, not mistakes).

I know as a basketball coach and teacher that as I evaluated each practice, game, and lesson, there was never one in which I could not have done a better job. I always go back to how my father lived: He did the best job he could do every day, until he died; he never had time to hate another person because he was trying to be the best person he could be.

I wish that I had his mentality. It would make my life easier if I could see past people's crusty exteriors and straight into their hearts.

How can you ever win someone over to your point of view if you build a wall between yourself and them? Without a wall, you might realize that your own point of view is off-center. Don't get me wrong, there are values that should never be compromised, but sometimes it is not about values—instead, it is about winning.

As Voltaire once said, "I do not agree with a word you say, but I will defend to death your right to say it." We should respect one another's opinions without conceding our own beliefs. Jesus did not preach, "If you don't agree with me, I'm going to send you straight to hell." Jesus fed the people, loved them, and lived by example.

If you don't agree with what I just said, please don't hate me.

Basketball-Cybernetics

When I first started coaching, the girls' coach at Trezevant High School, Richard Welch, had all of his players sit in the dressing room before a game with all the lights out and their eyes closed. They would visualize performing the basic fundamentals of the game; they would, in their minds' eyes, dribble, pass, shoot, and rebound for about ten minutes. He was a great coach and highly successful at a very small school, with a state championship to back it up.

I had a player who could literally jump over his car. Eric had at least a forty-five-inch vertical. The only problem was that he had hands of stone; they were hard, with little flexibility, and his hand-eye coordination was lacking. About that time, I heard through Coach Don Meyer of a book by Stan Kellner called *Basketball-Cybernetics*. I talked Coach Kellner into coming to our gym to promote his book and put on a demonstration. I invited every middle and high school coach and team in West Tennessee. Sadly, only about one-fourth attended.

Coach Kellner took ten random players from the crowd and had them jump at the rim or backboard and mark on their hands where they touched it. He then had them visualize jumping with a free and easy motion. Then, he told them to jump free and easy, giving it 95 percent effort. Each kid jumped from one to two inches higher.

I read his book that night, and the next day, I started with Eric. While everyone else was on the court, Eric would sit in the dressing room in the dark with his eyes closed and visualize catching all types of passes and rebounds; he would catch bounce passes, lobs, bad passes, and hard passes. There was immediate improvement. Eric wasn't ready to play shortstop for the St. Louis Cardinals, but he became an adequate catcher of the ball, and his confidence rose in other areas as well.

Other players have used cybernetics to improve their free-throw shooting with great success. Cybernetics is not a cure-all for inefficiencies, but it is definitely a tool.

Basketball-Cybernetics by Stan Kellner is a good read. While you are at it, go ahead and read *Psycho-Cybernetics* by Maxwell Maltz.

Candlesticks

Many years ago, I was watching a silly baseball movie—it could have been *Bull Durham* or *Major League*. All I remember about it was that the pitcher was struggling, and the coach came to the mound and asked what was the problem. The catcher spoke up and said the pitcher had to buy a wedding present and did not know what to buy. The coach said, "Candlesticks. Candlesticks always make a nice present," and walked back to the dugout. After that, the pitcher threw great.

What does this have to do with coaching basketball? Remember this: Things that are not important to you may be of tremendous importance to someone else. You have to know your kids, and they have to trust you enough to tell you what's bugging them and causing them to be distracted.

How do you build trust? One way is to talk to them during drills about school, life, and home when you think they are distracted. Take players home; this is a good way to understand their life outside the gym. Ask other teachers about their classroom behavior. Ask the leaders of the team to tell you when there is a potential problem.

Remember to let your players know you care about them as people and not only as players. At the same time, do not cross the line of being a buddy.

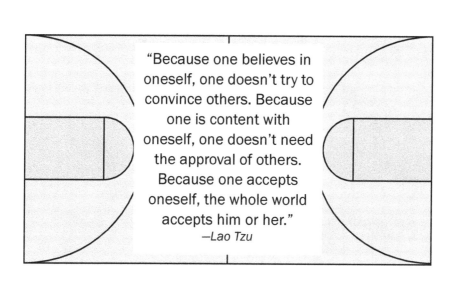

"Because one believes in oneself, one doesn't try to convince others. Because one is content with oneself, one doesn't need the approval of others. Because one accepts oneself, the whole world accepts him or her."
—*Lao Tzu*

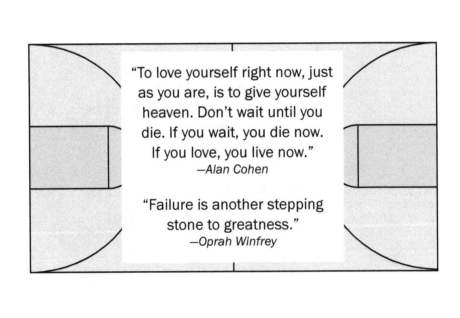

"To love yourself right now, just as you are, is to give yourself heaven. Don't wait until you die. If you wait, you die now. If you love, you live now."
—*Alan Cohen*

"Failure is another stepping stone to greatness."
—*Oprah Winfrey*

Collective Confidence

What is confidence? Why does it come and go? Can you have confidence in others and not in yourself? Can you have confidence in yourself and not in others? How do you teach confidence?

These are all questions that you must find the answers to each year as you and your teams grow together. The answers can be the same or different, depending on the personality of the team.

What is confidence?

Confidence is the quality within us that turns thoughts into actions. The more positive our thoughts are, the more positive our actions are.

Why does confidence come and go?

First, confidence comes from preparation and the memory of success. When we experience continued failure, we naturally doubt ourselves. If you teach proper technique and abundant repetition, you create muscle memory: Your brain will record the progress and should want to try it out. When you practice, you are instilling either good or bad habits. Don't let the little stuff slide. As John Wooden has been quoted so many times, "Practice doesn't make perfect. Perfect practice makes perfect."

Can you have confidence in others and not in yourself?

The truth is, we tend to overrate others' abilities and underrate our own. When you play a team that is more confident than yours, your players—no matter how they play—are always waiting on the other team to come and take them. I hear all the time that it is hard to beat a team three times. *REALLY?!* You are telling me that you would rather play a team that has beaten you three times? The truth is, you and your team know in the back of your minds that the other team is better than you.

Can you have confidence in yourself and not in others?

Basketball is the ultimate team sport. Players are totally dependent on each other for success. You can have star players, but for the team to be successful, the star player must make his teammates better. Michael Jordan is a great example of this. I have coached several players who have had supreme self-confidence but could not—or would not—raise the level of play in their teammates. This type of player is selfish and would rather be the star of the team than to make the team shine. How do you handle this type of player? I think good communication is the key: You should explain to him the problem and its solution, and you should explain to the team the problem and its solution.

How do you teach confidence?

Preparation through teaching proper technique is imperative. Don't overcook the execution; when you get it right, move on to the next drill. Don't do a drill until the players get tired and start messing up; just come back to it the next day or later in practice.

Success in practice will lead to success in the game. The old word "courage" comes back into play—the willingness to follow through no matter what.

Finally, a great team has collective confidence. This is when the team believes in what they are doing. The players believe in the coach's leadership. They are efficient and communicate well among themselves and with their coach. They believe the outcome is worth the effort. Simply said: Collective confidence means they have "bought in," and this always starts with leadership. If you have a cancer, remove it. If a cancer continues to pop up, you must re-evaluate yourself. There is nothing more rewarding than coaching a team with collective confidence.

I suggest you read works by Marianne Williamson. She believes that although we fear failure and inadequacy, our deepest fear is that we do not live up to our own adequacies. Someone once said that hell is dying and seeing the person you could have been. Keep that in mind.

"Our deepest fear is not that we are inadequate. Our deepest fear is that we are powerful beyond measure. It is our light, not our darkness, that most frightens us. We ask ourselves, 'Who am I to be brilliant, gorgeous, talented, fabulous?' Actually, who are you *not* to be? You are a child of God. Your playing small does not serve the world. There is nothing enlightened about shrinking so that people won't feel insecure around you. We are all meant to shine as children do. And as we let our own light shine, we are unconsciously giving others permission to do the same. As we are liberated from our own fears, our presence automatically liberates others."

—Marianne Williamson

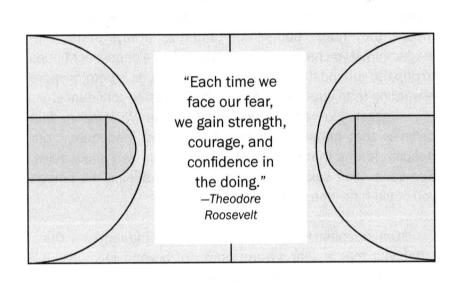

"Each time we
face our fear,
we gain strength,
courage, and
confidence in
the doing."
—*Theodore
Roosevelt*

Ownership

One of my favorite teams was from the 1984–85 season. The players were overachievers who worked hard and were very close. I knew they were special when, one day, I got called to the office for a phone call; I had to leave the gym and walk to the main office to take it. I gave my practice schedule to my point guard because I didn't have an assistant coach, and then I left. When I got back, I peeked through the gym doors for about twenty minutes and watched them go over three drills as hard as they could.

Needless to say, I realized this was their team. I walked in and stopped practice. We talked about the ownership of the team and how all of us owned this team. We became partners that day, but I was still the managing partner.

I introduced the flex offense to our team—and pretty much all of West Tennessee—in 1981. By 1985, we had all kinds of options. One night, we were playing some other team, and I noticed our players running back screens instead of down screens, and we were getting backdoor layups over and over. The other team called timeout, and I asked my players what they were doing. Rodney said that I told them to take ownership of the team.

What does ownership mean? First, the coach has to trust his players. Second, the players have to commit to the team more than to themselves. It means that if one player does badly, everyone does badly, and if one player does well, all players do well.

We were regular-season district champions, and not one player made the all-district team. We won the district championship, and two players were put on the all-district tournament team. When their names were announced, the whole team went out to receive the plaques. From this team, the starting seven are all great adults today. These players are also still close; they are more like brothers than teammates.

That season and that team taught me the importance of ownership and how giving up some of your own ego can open the door to greater understanding and achievement. This team's attitude was passed down to underclassmen who followed in their footsteps.

The Talk I Never Gave

In times of high anxiety, our emotions sometimes overwhelm our reasoning and common sense; our impulses can rule our thoughts. This can happen when it is of utmost importance for the coach to be the ship's anchor.

I had a great team who walked through the district, region, and sub-state. I did not see what was about to happen and had no plan for it. We had players arguing with their parents and each other. We had players probably doing things they should not have been doing. Basically, the worst in them came out. If I had a chance to do my job over again, I would have given them "The Talk."

Points of 'The Talk'

1. Have each player write down something good about each other, including themselves, on separate pieces of paper.

2. Have each player write down something about themselves and all the other players that they do not like on separate pieces

of paper. Take these papers, put them in a metal trash can, and burn it in front of them.

3. Tell the players that the worst in them has been destroyed— and that it's up to them to leave it destroyed or to create it all over again.

4. Give each of them the papers that said something good.

5. Ask them who they really are.

I was not the anchor; I failed my team. I can make all kinds of excuses, but it is my responsibility to be prepared for everything.

Never Never Means Never;
Always Never Means Always

I have always been a stickler for set offenses and set plays. When I started coaching, Bobby Knight's motion offense was in vogue. It dealt with reading and reacting to the defense. This seemed like a good idea, but in reality, my high school players did the same thing every time, no matter how the defense played. They moved more slowly because they were thinking instead of reacting.

I decided that if the players were going to do the same thing every time, they would do what I wanted and not what they wanted. So I put in set offenses and set plays. We broke the offenses down into parts and worked on proper techniques. There are still reads within set offenses, such as going over or under screens, backdoors, curls, and flares. My main rule was "Never never means never, and always never means always." Because breakdowns in offense and defense call for specific reads, you should never say things like, "Always go under the screens" if the defense goes under the screen. You get the idea.

Players should have the freedom to react to what the defense or offense is doing, but first they must understand the parameters of the defense or offense. Players cannot be allowed to do their own things; they must understand how important cohesiveness is to the team offense. At the same time, you want players to be alert to situations such as overplays, double teams, mismatches, and out-of-position defenses.

Even though we ran set plays, I had an offense called Nike. Many years ago, Nike had a commercial that said, "Just do it." In Nike, the players had no set offense. The rule was that you could not stand in the same place for more than two seconds. After two seconds, you had to either cut or set a screen. Because we were constantly setting and using screens in our set offense, the players knew what to do. So I guess Nike was a motion offense. It was fun, and the players enjoyed using their own creativity.

Never Be Mad When You Are Mad

There is a big difference between being perturbed and being mad. When you are perturbed, you stop practice and run or do whatever is needed to get your point across. When you are mad, you are ready to overreact and do or say something that you will regret later. I learned that when I was mad in practice, I needed to stop what we were doing and do some sort of fun team drill, such as dribble tag, until I got back to the right frame of mind.

Is it good for your players to see you mad? Absolutely. But use it to your advantage: Use it as an attention-getter. I would put on my practice schedule the exact time that I would go off. It usually resulted in throwing a ball against the wall, backboard, or floor. I would yell at the team, not an individual. I would let them know that something was not acceptable. We would then do something until it was done right; we might work on checking out, getting through picks, communicating, or executing a play. Sometimes, I would repeatedly say, "You are better than this!"

The Definition of Misery

There is nothing more miserable than having a player on your team, with or without talent, who doesn't want to be there. Most of the time, he is being pushed to be on the team by one or both of his parents. He may be burnt out by youth leagues and travel ball. He has lost his passion for the game. I have seen so many of these kids who never picked up a ball again after their high school (or sometimes middle school) careers ended.

Some kids have enough ability to play, but their heart is in something else. It could be music, another sport, or another activity. I believe that some kids can handle multiple undertakings, and others do not have the talent or drive. Some kids are natural multitaskers and can excel in many areas while others do better at doing one thing at a time.

As a coach, you have to keep the lines of communication open with all your players; you must invest in them to understand them. In the end, a player without love and passion for the game will hurt the team. By his senior year, he will be a cancer to the team. He could be a good kid, but unmotivated kids do not motivate others.

As a result, the kid is miserable because he would rather be somewhere else; the coach is miserable because he can't get the most out of the player; the rest of the team is miserable because the player's body language and interactions with them are negative; and the parents are miserable because the coach did not make their child the star they wanted him to be. I can only imagine the dinner conversations.

That being said, I do not cut seniors. If the unmotivated player has a good attitude, he will probably quit the team to make room for someone who is passing him by.

Why Some Coaches Stop Coaching and Others Don't

Do coaches stop coaching because they don't love the game anymore? Is it because of the crazy parents or lack of talent year after year? Do they burn out from all the long hours and little pay? Or is it because of family responsibilities? Could it be because the dream of being a major college coach is just not going to happen?

These are all reasons that coaches get out of coaching. So what are the reasons that some of them coach until they die or are physically unable to continue? Some coaches, including me, just never grow up. Some need to continually refill their egos. Some coach for the extra money. Some coach because that is all they have ever done. But there are some who coach for excellence; they want to be the best they can be so that when the young coaches go to coaching clinics, they will see the experienced coaches there hoping to pick up a thing or two they can use.

These coaches still have passion. They use basketball

as a tool to teach young men and women to be successful, well-adjusted adults. They usually have wives or husbands beside them with a passion for the sport created by their love for their spouse. You might see their kids and grandkids in the huddle or crowd, urging the team on. The team becomes their family in an aunt-and-uncle sort of way.

These coaches find colleges for the players capable of playing at that level. They find jobs for the other players. When a player fails at something, these coaches take it personally and try to get the player on the right track. Then, for some strange reason, Father Time catches up with the coaches when they have lived a productive and fruitful life.

If you are a young coach, my advice to you is this: Basketball is a tool to help build young people into the people God wants them to be, but you have to live this life with integrity if you want the kids to buy in totally.

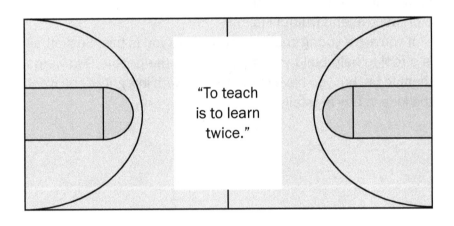

"To teach
is to learn
twice."

Coaching the Injured Player

For a teacher, knowledge of the subject matter is only the beginning. You must be able to apply your knowledge and information in a way that can be understood and used by your students. If you cannot do this, everyone, including you, will become frustrated and disenchanted. The same is true in coaching. It doesn't matter how much you know or how well you can do it; all that matters is whether the players can grasp the techniques and apply them. This brings me to my thoughts on how to coach the injured player.

A player's worst nightmare is injury, especially a knee injury. You must remember that teenagers think they are invincible, and when they realize they are not, it can be devastating to their psyche. This means that not only must they heal physically, but they must heal mentally as well.

I have found the best way to handle an injured player is to keep him involved in all aspects of the game. Don't waste his time. Make him an assistant coach. Let him in on staff meetings.

Let him run drills. Ask him for advice. Give him responsibilities during the game, such as keeping a difficult stat or charting passes. Have him summarize the stats. Let him have a five- to ten-minute segment in the practice plan.

By taking all of these steps—or some of them—you have kept your injured player involved. There is nothing worse than having an injured player lying on the bleachers asleep during practice. His apathy can spread to the whole team; he is miserable, you are miserable looking at him, and the players are miserable listening to him feel sorry for himself.

When the injured player is involved, he is touching the ball and interacting with players and coaches, so when he comes back from his injury, he is more prepared to step into his role on the team without as much reteaching. As a coach, you have let the team know that you care about all the players, not just the ones who matter on the court right now. You will also have a player who will appreciate you and be a loyal friend for life.

Coaching the Superstar

It was once said that the only person who could stop Michael Jordan from scoring was his own coach, Dean Smith. The key is not to let a star player become a prima donna; you must expect your best player to work as hard or harder than the rest of the team. Show him examples of players with great attitudes and their successes.

Help these players understand how the public wants to be part of their lives and the distraction and temptation these people will create. I shall never forget winning the district championship against one of the state's best teams who had the best player in the state. One of our fans won a $1,000 bet on that game. That was a Saturday night, and we had to play the first region game on Monday afternoon. This fan took our two star players out partying after the game. We practiced on Sunday afternoon, and both were visibly sick. They played miserably on Monday, and I was criticized horribly for our loss. I found out a few months later what had happened. Our team was good enough to win the state championship, but one short-sighted decision ended that dream.

I never saw this coming, but I learned from it. After that, I spent a lot more time driving home "the right way to do things."

When the best player on the team works harder than everyone else, you will have good team chemistry. Sha Brooks is a perfect example of a star player with a great work ethic. We had to take her out of a lot of drills because she would blow them up with her instinct, ability, speed, and hustle. There was some jealousy, but the players respected her more than they envied her ability. Sha went on to become All-State for four straight years, All-Southeastern Conference at Florida, and drafted thirty-second in the WNBA. She has had a long and fabulous career in Europe.

Try to treat the star player the same as the fifteenth player on the team. Teach him to compliment and play up his teammates' accomplishments. He will be interviewed a lot more than the rest of the team, so you must teach him to use this to build up the team. Explain to him what coaches want and don't want in a player. And, most important, don't let him slack in the classroom. If he doesn't respond the right way, show him that no one is too good to sit on the bench. Accept nothing but his best.

Beware of your best player wearing different-colored shoes, socks, etc. I've been told that I was too old-school about this, but my players dressed exactly the same on the court. Either everyone wore T-shirts under their uniforms or no one did; their socks, shoes, and wristbands were bought by the school. The captain of the team would wear the patch on his warm-up but not on his uniform; he would get to keep his warm-up after the season.

My rules were simple: Act right or I will deal with it. This is so hard to do today because of sports entertainment and "let the kids play." We coaches need to remember that almost all of these kids will have to get a job someday, so they need to have the work ethic, self-discipline, and ability to work with others in order to succeed in the workplace.

Coaching the Introvert

I have coached several talented, extreme introverts. As a younger coach, I did a terrible job understanding and motivating them. I was hard on them, and the harder I was, the more they crawled into their shells; the more they crawled into their shells, the more I yelled at them. It took a special player and team to teach me how to do better.

Stacy was a great practice and preseason player, but the closer it got to the season, the worse he played. I felt like I used him as a whipping boy sometimes. Why he tolerated me was a testament to his love for the game. Between his junior and senior year, I noticed how his teammates encouraged him and how his body language began to change. I started telling him how much he had improved and how proud I was of him. I moved him outside to a guard position, and he took off. I still demanded a lot out of him, but I guess we both grew up a little.

Stacy had a great senior year, and our team had a fabulous season. Today, he is one of the nicest and most hardworking people you could ever meet. A coach himself now, he has won the 4A state championship in Indiana girls basketball and is a threat to win it every year.

I have had several other players since then who were introverts. Each one had a great senior year; the difference between them and Stacy was that I didn't make them miserable in their earlier years. I have learned to appeal to their intellect and reasoning skills and help them understand themselves.

The Player With ADD

Another kind of player is the extreme ADD player. First, you must understand what ADD is. It is not the inability to focus, but it is the inability to *stay* focused. Almost everything is a distraction—any kind of noise or movement. The key is to eliminate as many distractions as possible and to train the player to refocus as quickly as possible.

Andy had this problem, and the more I got on him, the worse he performed. My assistant coach, Larry Jones, asked me why I was spending so much time on Andy, who didn't play much, instead of the starters. I went home and pondered the question: Why *did* I spend so much time on Andy?

The next day, I ignored Andy's mistakes and concentrated on my starters. The result was this: My starters played better; there was less tension in practice; the team's chemistry came together; and Andy got better, becoming an important player on the team.

Three Kinds of Attitudes

There are three kinds of attitudes: good, bad, and wrong.

A player with a good attitude puts the team first, works hard, invests in the team, and oozes positive energy. A player with a bad attitude is the opposite: He is selfish, does no more than he has to do, is the first one out the door, and is the last one into the gym. A player with the wrong attitude is usually misguided. He might be getting too much coaching from home; he might have a problem with total commitment. He might really care but is unable to control his emotions; or he argues, gets mad easily, and pouts. As a coach, you have to make it clear what a good attitude is and accept nothing less.

I have had more than my share of kids with great attitudes. Kevin couldn't jump, wasn't quick, and was an above-average shooter. We weren't highly talented, and Kevin had to play out of position. Once, at just a little over six feet tall, he had to guard a seven-footer. He never complained; he was, and is, a great young man. He is extremely conscientious and intelligent.

Kevin became a successful college baseball player and has spent the rest of his life as a talented teacher and coach. Players with bad attitudes didn't last long enough with me to write about them.

Another Kevin who played for me had a wrong attitude. He had a bad temper. He learned to turn his anger into energy and was one of the toughest kids I ever coached. Today, he works hard as a coach himself on the high school level.

No Regrets

One of my favorite players was Larry Hicks. I came to Crockett County High School after ten years at Bolivar. I was not sure what I had gotten into: We had a lot of talent but not a lot of discipline. The first day of practice, we had thirty kids. The second day, sixteen showed up. Those sixteen kids bought in, and they went from two wins the previous year to twenty-three wins under me. The next season was twenty-six wins and a trip to the sub-state, where we had a one-point loss to a stunning Memphis team.

The leader of the Crockett team was Larry, without a doubt. Larry refused to lose. He was our six-foot-tall center who averaged over one dunk per game. He wasn't the fastest player on the team, but he would dive across the finish line to win a sprint. The turning point came about one-third of the way through that first season. We were playing Trenton Peabody and made an incredible comeback. With about thirty seconds left in the game, we cut the lead to one point. Trenton Peabody couldn't get the ball inbounds, and their player called a timeout that the team didn't have, resulting in a two-shot technical foul and the ball. I asked who wanted to shoot the free throws, and Larry piped up, "I'm shooting the free throws!" Now, Larry wasn't our best free-throw shooter, but I had no doubt he would make them, which he did. We then scored on the inbounds play. Then we scored again. We never looked back after that game.

I'll never forget the last game in which I coached Larry and the team. We lost to Memphis Treadwell. After the game, the players were crying, all except for Larry. I couldn't take it and walked outside the dressing room. Larry hugged each of the players, then walked outside to me with the biggest smile, hugged me, and said, "It's been fun, Coach."

Everyone can look back at their life and see things they wish they had done differently. I don't think Larry could do that when it came to how he played basketball. While we all subconsciously feel that if we had tried harder here or there, outcomes might have been different, Larry gave his best every day, without exception.

Larry had no regrets—that's why he had no tears to shed.

He went on to make the Class AA all-state team.

Dealing With a Rogue Player

For a rogue player to make the team, he must love basketball more than he loves being stupid. Use his love to control him; be clear what you expect and will not tolerate. The advantage of this player is that if he is guided the right way, he tends to play with no fear. The disadvantage is that he may return to his rogue ways and take others with him.

One way to develop this player is to give him responsibilities. You must "trust but verify" him in class: Check with students you trust about his behavior. It's okay if the rogue player knows you are checking on him. This lets him know that you are serious and you care.

When I started coaching, I was an assistant under Mark Massey at Adamsville High School; I learned so much from him in two years. One player there, Garland, was a perfect example of a rogue player: He brought an attitude to school with him, but he was likable and intelligent. Coach Massey made him captain of the team and met with him a lot for Garland to report on the status of the team. Garland felt special and did a fabulous job—he took ownership of the team. He—and we—had a great year.

Notice I used the word "he" and not "they." You do not want two rogue players on the same team. They have a tendency to pull each other down.

The Fifteenth Player on the Team

You must convince the fifteenth player on the team to be the best fifteenth player in the league. Believe me: The players know their order by play and practice time. They must be engaged because engagement starts at both ends and meets in the middle. The players on the end of the bench must be monitored as well.

How to do it:

■ Sit in the middle of the bench instead of at the end.

■ Video the bench during free throws and timeouts.

■ Have your wife or assistant coach sit behind the bench.

■ When you take the team to places, sit with all the players—not just your favorites. You may not think you have favorites, but you do; it's human nature.

■ Don't run up scores and not put everyone in.

■ Don't embarrass a player by putting him in the last few seconds of a game.

Coaching Stories and Opinions

The predicament

I was told the following story by Jimmy Geans, former coach at Adamsville High School:

At a 1960s coaches' meeting, Coach Calhoun of Bethel Springs High School explained a predicament that he had: He had finished practicing his high school girls team and thought everyone had left, so he went into the dressing room to turn out the lights. When he walked in, his best player, who happened to be beautiful, walked out of the shower with nothing on and explained that she had been waiting for him.

Coach Calhoun explained to the other coaches that he told her to put her clothes on, and he would pretend this had never happened. Then he asked the other coaches what they would have done. That is when Coach Geans said that he would have done exactly the same thing. Coach Calhoun, with a sigh of relief, said, "You would?" and Coach Geans said, "Absolutely. I would have lied about it, too."

I told this story to illustrate to coaches that once you do something morally wrong with a player, you can't undo it. As Brother Charles Stanley often reminds me, "You reap what you sow, more than you sow, later than you sow."

T. E. Chisholm

McNairy County, Tennessee, consolidated its small high schools of Ramer, Michie, Selmer, Bethel Springs, and Adamsville into one school called McNairy Central in 1969, the year I graduated. Adamsville refused to give up its school and even tried to get the county boundaries changed. Finally, after two years of arguments, Adamsville got to keep its school. The school board decided to open enrollment, and they made T. E. Chisholm the principal.

Mr. Chisholm was a mammoth of a man with a violent temper. He had been the boys' basketball coach and was good but was feared by all. The school board members thought the Adamsville students would choose to go to the shiny, new school over the rundown AHS that had a domineering principal. Little did they know that God had another plan. Mr. Chisholm started going to church with his wonderful wife and was led to Christ. He proved to be a loving and smart principal, and the school flourished. Adamsville became one of the best schools in the state, and many kids, because of open enrollment, came from outside the city to go to Adamsville. AHS became financially independent because of Aqua Glass and other industries.

Mr. Chisholm had the ability to recognize and hire good teachers. He was quite good at building teachers up and encouraging them to be the best they could be.

One of Mr. Chisholm's first hurdles to overcome was the school's horrific football team. Back then, there was no classification, and most small schools didn't have a team, so AHS had to play much larger schools. During the 1960s, AHS set the state record for the most consecutive losses. After one of the worst losses in history to the state powerhouse that was Brownsville High School, the entire team decided to quit the following Monday. Mr. Chisholm got wind of what was going to happen. Outside the football fieldhouse, there was a light pole lying on the ground with the players sitting on it, waiting on the coach to unlock the door so they could tell him they were quitting and turn in their equipment.

Mr. Chisholm sauntered up to the boys and said, "Boys, I hear that y'all are thinking of quitting. Well, we don't have no quitters around here." Then he pulled out a .22 revolver, emptied it across the field, and walked away. Not one player quit that day. Saving the football team was a pivotal part of saving the school.

Referees

You may find this hard to believe, but some of my best friends are referees, and some of the people I respect the most are referees. When I first started coaching, I got way more than my share of technicals. I wanted every call, and I felt that I didn't get any breaks. As I grew older, videotape became available, and I realized I was wrong a lot of the time.

I do believe that the old referees in particular were not going to automatically crown me, as a young, intense coach, the "King of Coaching." They were good at "T"-ing me up when we were on offense so the other team not only shot two free throws but got the ball as well.

Becoming a baseball umpire helped me appreciate referees more; it helped me understand how split-second decisions must be made and that sometimes your eyes or brain lock up on you. By the end of my career, I rarely got a technical foul because when I disagreed with the refs, I didn't show them up. I tried not to stare a referee down. I never used foul language and never went after them when the game was over. I remember more than once a referee telling me when I fussed about a call or missed call that he must have missed it because I never fussed for no reason. I don't know if that was a psychological ploy, but either way, it showed respect and, in turn, I gave respect back.

I have had a few interesting referee encounters, especially as a young coach. In 1980, I had a good player who was a 90 percent free-throw shooter. Every time we got fouled on the defensive end, he would be the free-throw shooter on the other end, whether it was he or someone else who got fouled. I didn't stop him, which I should have. He did this the entire season. One night when he did this, I looked at the referee, who was a great referee, and his face was so red that I knew we were caught. I immediately stood up and called timeout. He shook his head and handed the ball to my player, then called a technical foul. Next, he turned to me and gave me the timeout with a big grin on his face and said, "Gotcha."

Another time, we were playing at Lexington High School. One of the officials that night was also a great ref and a no-nonsense guy on the court. I told my players not to make eye contact with him, not to say anything to him, and always hand him the ball. In turn, I would physically sit on my hands. In the second quarter, my point guard was called for a blocking foul. He tapped the referee on the butt and said, "Good call." I immediately got a sub up for him, but it was too late. The referee would not let him in; he immediately called an offensive foul on my player and still did not let the sub in.

Then the referee called a defensive foul on my player. Then, with the first smile I had ever seen on him, he allowed the sub in. I told my player that it was his fault because he didn't do what I had told him.

Another incident occurred when I was a young coach, and they used a two-man crew. We were playing a strong team and had a small lead near the end of the game. We had spread the court in our four-corner offense. My player caught a pass and landed with the edge of his foot barely touching the sideline, right in front of the scorers' table. Their coach yelled and pointed at the line. The referee was across the court, and it was impossible for him to see it, but he called it anyway. As he was inbounding the ball right in front of me, I asked, "Did you see it, or did the other coach talk you into the call?"

The referee shot back, "Are you questioning my integrity?"

And I said, "What is this, a civil service test?" That's when he "T"-ed me up.

I believe that all coaches should officiate another sport. It would help alleviate the officiating shortage, and coaches would realize how hard officiating really is. It would help to keep good officials interacting with each other and other coaches.

I Don't Know How They Do It

How do coaches talk to the media after a tough loss? I have a hard time talking before the game, but I'm not a pleasant person after a loss.

After an emotional win, I have way too much adrenaline flowing, and I am apt to say something about an incident during the game that I might regret later. After a loss, the human tendency is to blame something or someone, but if you are smart, you can use the media to your advantage.

One of the most talented players I ever coached was six feet six inches tall with long arms and big hands. He was an incredible athlete with one major problem: He played up and down according to the talent level of the team we were playing. In the semifinals of the regional tournament, we rolled over the team we played, thanks to everyone but him. His stats were something in the range of four points and two rebounds. The media approached me after the game. I praised my other players and how they bailed out my star player. In the championship game, he had a triple-double with twenty-four points, twenty rebounds, and ten blocked shots; he even made an unbelievable blocked shot to secure the victory.

Another incident took place at a school where I had coached for a couple of years. Our school was sandwiched between two larger schools that had dominated for more than twenty years; one had the second leading scorer in the state behind the legendary Tony Delk. We beat them in our gym in convincing fashion. We had sold Coca-Colas in paper cups at the concession stand, and after the game, their fans pelted us with them.

Their local newspaper covered both teams. The reporter asked me how we won, and I said that they shot like their fans threw paper cups—they couldn't hit anything. I wish I hadn't said it, but it sounded good at the time. It did help to re-create a fierce rivalry that had been lacking. It made a lot of money for both schools. After that night, there were full-capacity crowds in both gyms.

Another incident occurred when we played a private school in our district. I had scouted them and recognized that they had a dirty player on their team. I saw him undercut one player and later sucker-punch another.

We played them in our gym, and during the game, one of my players came to me complaining that this particular player had hit him in the face. I checked the film and, sure enough, it happened. They beat us in every way that night. The newspaper asked me about the game and the team the next day, and my response was: "They are a talented and very well-coached dirty-white-boy team that tries to intimidate."

Well, when we came to their gym and ran out to warm up, music started playing. It was "Dirty White Boy" by Foreigner. Every time the lyric "dirty white boy" came up in the song, their fans pointed at me and screamed, "Dirty white boy!"

Long story short, I was fired up and so were our kids. We

won in convincing fashion. After the game, their coach, who is a good man, pulled the article out of his pocket and shoved it in my face. I asked him if he was going to show it to me if he had won. He said probably not. We both walked away, but the rivalry was on.

One of the hardest things I have ever done as a coach is a postgame interview after a season-ending loss at the state tournament. People don't realize that when you lose that last game, it's like someone close to you has died; you have put so much into the season, and it is over. There is an immediate void that is almost overwhelming. It takes me several weeks to adjust and function properly again. All you can do is take that season and use it to motivate you and your team for the next season.

That New Car Smell

There's something special about the smell of a new car. A friend of mine trades cars every year just because he loves that "new car smell" so much. If you are ever fortunate enough to own a new car, you will probably hand-wash it twice a week; no one will be allowed to eat in it. You will probably park a mile away from the front door of Walmart so that no one will park next to you.

As the new car smell gradually fades away, so does your meticulousness; you will start running it through the car wash once a month and going through the drive-through at McDonald's, and you will circle the parking lot to find a closer spot to park.

I fear coaches get caught up in the new car smell as well. That first practice is meticulously planned. The practice schedule covers everything. As the season wears on, though, practices become stale and less organized. Things are taken for granted. There's an old saying: "If you're not prepared for practice once, you will know it; twice, and your players will know it; and if you're not prepared three times, everyone will know it."

To be accountable, you must keep that new car smell. If not, you might find yourself getting traded in for a newer model. Practice must continue to accomplish goals and objectives each and every day. One way to make sure this happens is to use games you have just played and are going to play to determine what you work on. Have a manager on the bench with a notebook: Every time you see something wrong during the game, have them make a note of it.

Another way to keep your new car smell is to make drills short and intense.

Remember that there should be a purpose for every drill, such as:

■ To get ready for the next game.
■ To get better fundamentally.
■ To create good chemistry.
■ To prepare for that team down the road that you must defeat to get where you want to be.
■ To teach your players to be good teammates and good people.

Practice is sacred, and every minute should be of value. You don't want to look back at the season and say, "We should have worked harder in practice." Your last practice should be better than your first. If not, you haven't improved as a coach, and you don't know your team well enough.

You know, that new car smell can also apply to your job as a teacher, your family relationships, and your relationship with your Savior. Why not have a good lesson plan? Why not find better ways to do your job? Why not make your family feel special? And why not get closer to your Savior?

AAU and Travel Ball

The strengths of AAU and travel ball as I see them are:
■ You get to play against good competition most of the time.
■ Just playing makes you better.
■ If you are an elite player, you get to showcase your talent in front of college coaches and scouts.

AAU and travel ball also have a lot of weaknesses, such as:
■ Many coaches are wannabes.
■ Many teams are created to showcase the coaches' sons or players from a certain team.
■ Games are poorly officiated, which encourages bad shots, poor defense, and illegal footwork.
■ AAU and travel ball encourage individual play over team play.

My great fear is that basketball is becoming a game of shallow entertainment in which dunks, three-pointers, and blocked shots are all that matter. I fear that self-discipline and the art of the game are not important anymore.

I can remember working on direct drives, crossovers, jump stops, and forward and reverse pivots on a daily basis. I watch NBA games, and there is no such thing as a pivot foot or step-and-a-half layup. This works its way down to the Eurostep, which is a step and a half, then a crossover step, then another step before you shoot a layup.

How is someone supposed to guard this without fouling?

Checking out is another fundamental that has gone by the wayside for most teams because of the Eurostep and blocked shot. Villanova won the NCAA national championship in 2016 and 2018, and Virginia won in 2019 because they are the best two teams in college basketball when it comes to checking out.

It takes self-discipline to do your job and be fundamental. What is wrong with teaching kids self-discipline? What upsets me most is that ESPN and other sports stations have pushed the sport into a game of entertainment and athleticism. Are we teaching our players that doing the little things on and off the court is a waste of time?

How important are winning and losing? When you play fifty or more travel or AAU games during the summer, you get used to losing, and losing becomes no big deal. Winning becomes commonplace as well.

When the high school regular season starts, the team might be in midseason form with no place to go but to become flat and complacent. Players can burn out and not be able to wait for the season to end.

You should spend a few weeks working on skills or hold a summer camp, and then let the kids do summer stuff. This way they can develop other muscles, enjoy their family, and have a fresh mind when school starts back.

Lessons From My Daddy

My father died of a heart attack when I was twenty-four years old. He was sixty-three. He didn't talk a lot, but he said so many things with his actions.

His father came to America from England with his family when he was a little boy in the 1880s. He grew up to be just like his father and grandfather—an alcoholic with no education and no skill. My grandfather could not read or write and signed his name with an X. My grandmother suffered from severe asthma and died in her forties.

My dad only went to school when there was a basketball or baseball game. He finally dropped out of school in the seventh grade at age seventeen. He spent most of his time trapping mink and muskrats for their hides to support the family. By age fourteen, he was well on his way to becoming like his father and grandfather, but God entered in: My father fell out of a wagon while he was drunk and hit his head on a rock. He was unconscious for more than two weeks. When he woke up, to everyone's surprise, he was saved. From that point on, he never drank another drop of alcohol, said a curse word, or said a negative thing about another human being.

My father and mother married when he was twenty-one and she was twenty in 1935. They had four children: James Kelly, who was fourteen years older than me; Donald Ray, who was nine years older than me; me; and my sister Annitta, who was three years younger than me. They sharecropped for a living. They had sixteen dollars when they got married and paid five dollars a month for their house. They woke one morning after a snowstorm, and their bed was covered with snow.

In 1940, my dad borrowed five hundred dollars from the richest man in the area and bought an eighty-acre farm. He cut the timber and paid the loan back that winter. He was never in debt again. He built the house I was raised in and then bought another farm. He raised as many as a thousand hogs at a time and always had time for his kids.

Things I learned from my father
■ He never repeated himself. You had better listen and get it the first time.
■ He would always show you how to do things. You had better observe and get it.
■ He always washed up and wore a clean shirt at the dinner table. Not doing this was disrespecting my mother.
■ Children were not allowed to talk at the dinner table without permission.
■ He never quit anything until it was finished right.

Learning by example
My oldest brother, James Kelly, sat next to my second brother, Donald Ray, at the dinner table. James Kelly was picking at Donald Ray under the table, and Donald Ray was getting mad.

My daddy sat at the end next to James Kelly. He took his left arm and backhanded James Kelly so hard that he and his chair flipped over backward. No one said a word; James Kelly got up, sat back down, and we finished eating.

Donald Ray was the black sheep of the family. He was always trying to get out of work, and he liked to stay out late with his girlfriend. Daddy never told us when to get home, but we all knew that we got up at five every morning to feed the animals before breakfast.

Daddy had Donald Ray plowing all night in the back field. He was seventeen years old and about to graduate from high school. About eight o'clock that night, my daddy and I walked to the field to check on him.

Donald Ray had pulled up in the corner of the field and was propped up against the back wheel of the tractor, sound asleep. My daddy went to the ditch bank and cut a sapling about four feet long. He woke Donald Ray up, whipping him. Donald Ray was about six feet two inches tall and more than 200 pounds, and Daddy was maybe five feet nine inches tall and 160 pounds, so Donald Ray decided to fight back. When Daddy got through with him, all he had left in his hand of that four-foot sapling was about four inches. My brother plowed until he ran out of gas around four in the morning.

On the way back to the house, I told my daddy that I would never disobey him again, and I kept my word. This all might seem harsh, but our livelihood depended on our crops, and Donald Ray chose sleep over the family. His decision to stay out late the night before was selfish, and that was unacceptable.

My father never once told me that he loved me; that's not what people of the Depression era did. But he showed me his love every day by teaching me how to use my brain and my hands. He demonstrated humility, honesty, determination, and a strong work ethic. He did this with a "you can do it" attitude.

My First Day of School

I was five years old and starting the first grade. There was no kindergarten back then. When lunchtime came for the first, second, and third grades, we all lined up, went to the cafeteria, and sat down until it was our turn to get those noisy aluminum trays for our food. Other students had their trays of food and were lined up to be seated by the teacher.

Harry Melton, a third-year first-grader, asked if I wanted to have some fun, and I said, "Sure." He told me to crawl under the table and trip the kids in line. It seemed like a good idea at the time, so I did. This created a chain reaction, and several kids fell on each other like dominoes. Mrs. Vaughan grabbed me up, slapped me in the face, and sat me down.

That day, our class was split between the smart kids and dumb kids, and I was put with the dumb kids. I'm sure my behavior had something to do with it, but mostly it was because I stuttered.

That afternoon, we loaded up on the buses. The buses were

lined up beside each other, about three feet apart. Right before they pulled out, Donald Ray, who was a freshman, and the other high school boys (who sat in the back of the bus so they could smoke) passed me out of the window onto the bus beside ours just as they pulled out. When Harlan McCoy parked his bus at home, he was surprised to find a passenger. He asked who I was and if I knew my phone number, and I explained what had happened and that we didn't have a telephone. So he loaded me up in his car and took me home.

Donald Ray wasn't any better than I was about thinking things through. We both got a good whipping for the decisions we made that day.

I was stuck in the slow class until the third grade. Ms. Henry and Mr. Littlefield, my speech teacher, helped me realize my potential. Ms. Henry had me read in front of the class on her knee without stuttering. It was one of the most positive things that happened to me.

Other Stories From My Youth

Where were you when it happened?

I will never forget the afternoon of November 22, 1963. I was in the seventh grade at Ramer School. We were playing an afternoon basketball game at Michie School. Back then, they let the entire school come to junior high games. I was shooting a free throw when an announcement came over the public address system, which I couldn't understand because of the crowd noise.

All of a sudden, all of the high school students started yelling and cheering. I looked over at our coach, Mr. Stanfield, and he had his head in his hands, crying. The first chance I got, I asked Mr. Stanfield what had happened, and he said that President Kennedy had been killed. I asked why everyone was so happy. He said, "I don't know."

Mr. Stanfield was on one of the battleships that were sunk at Pearl Harbor on December 7, 1941. He was injured serving his country.

Stupid things I did

Some stupid things I did as a kid were:

■ Bronco riding our cattle.

■ Climbing small trees and having my neighbor chop them down with an ax.

■ Jumping out of the back of the truck with my feet running, thinking that when I hit the ground I would not fall.

■ Shooting my brother between the eyes with my Daisy BB gun for picking on me.

■ Tying Ronnie Shea to the grapevine just before we were called in from recess.

■ Jumping off the car shed's roof onto my homemade seesaw to throw my little sister into the air.

We had a grove of woods next to our house with two gigantic oaks close to each other. Donald Ray and our neighbors had built treehouses in both and attached a rope in the top of one of them to swing from one treehouse to the other. They made bows and arrows out of saplings, tied me to the rope, and swung me from one tree to the other as they shot at me.

Needless to say, I was a physically and mentally tough kid by the time I got to high school.

The haybarn

My freshman year of high school was 1965–66. We were the first school in West Tennessee to have an integrated basketball team. Ramer High School in McNairy County, Tennessee, had won two state championships in 1928 and 1932. In 1959, Ramer was ranked No. 1 in the state. James Arthur Horton was the leading scorer in the nation and an All-American. Slick McMahan was a great scorer as well. Both were guards, and sometimes they would argue over who would throw the ball in because the other would usually shoot it. They once scored 100 points between them in a single game.

After 1959, Ramer went through some mediocre seasons. My freshman year, 1965, we became the first school in West Tennessee to integrate our basketball team. Thanks to Eddie Patterson and Andrew Ratliff, as well as Babo Smith, Steve Plunk, and Larry Horton (the younger brother of James Arthur), we won the county championship and were runner-up in the district. The regional tournament was in the Mid-South Coliseum in Memphis, and we had never played in anything but small, cracker-box gyms. I will never forget that, as we walked into the Coliseum, Eddie Patterson turned to Coach Williams and said, "Coach, I wonder how many bales of hay we could get in here." It was almost like a scene from *Hoosiers*, except we lost to a good team.

Payback

During my freshman year, I got my first bit of education in racism. One of our first away games was at Pickwick South Side. We walked into the dressing room, and hanging from a noose was a papier-mâché black person that had just been set on fire. Needless to say, my black brothers didn't play well that night. The referees that night called a foul or travel violation every time we did anything. We were soundly defeated.

We played them again much later in the season at Ramer, and we defeated them by almost 100 points. Coach Williams never subbed the entire night. I didn't get to play, but even at that time, I understood that justice had been served.

How not to have a second date

I will never forget my first date. It was 1967; I was fifteen years old and had my driver's permit. The date was with Judy Kirk, who was pretty and sweet. I picked her up at her family's house. As I was backing out of her driveway, I ran off the bridge over the ditch in her front yard, and I had to walk to Mr.

Stanfield's house to get him to pull us out of the ditch with his tractor.

We went to a drive-in picture show. I was so nervous the entire night that when the show was over, I forgot to take the speaker out of the car and pulled it from its frame.

Obviously, I didn't bother to ask her out again.

Knee Injuries and Stretching

I am convinced that the unbelievable increase in MCL and ACL tears is because kids don't ride bicycles anymore. If you want to be creative, go to yard sales and buy some old bikes to use in your preseason conditioning program. Buy one or two stationary bikes, too. These bikes are great to condition the lower body for players with upper-body injuries.

Other reasons for knee injuries are the shoes and the courts. When I played, we wore Chuck Taylors. Today's shoes and courts have too much traction. Courts have more coats of finish and are kept much cleaner than they were years ago. Because of the gripping shoes and well-kept floors, we must concentrate on strengthening the knees.

Stretching

The first time I tore a muscle was in 1974 after our coach put us on the Mitch Kupchak stretching program. I think warming up and light stretching are good, especially as you get older.

Cooling down and hanging from a bar upside-down can also be a good thing.

I'm convinced that overstretching can cause muscle fibers to weaken and pop. There are basically, as I understand, two types of muscle fibers—long, white ones and short, dark ones. For an athlete, the long fibers make you faster, and the short fibers make you quicker. These fibers are like rubber bands: If you overstretch them continuously, they can lose their elasticity and snap.

Being stronger is a good thing, but bulk, especially around the neck, can hinder the player's flexibility. Remember, a basketball player has his hands and arms above his head shooting and rebounding a lot.

The most important thing an AD should do

I coached at several schools, and in most of them, the coaches put their teams and programs above all else. Some coaches would not let their players participate in other sports; other coaches discouraged players by telling them that other players would pass them if they played another sport.

This is the most selfish, unprofessional attitude a coach can have. He has put his sport over the school, the kids, and the purpose of sport itself!

Approximately one in thirty thousand kids will be good enough to play professional sports, so let the kids determine what sports they want to play. Don't take the fun out of it. There are not many great athletes in most schools, and if they are allowed to play only one sport, the other sports will suffer. That's like telling someone who is good in math that they shouldn't learn English or science!

Another reason kids should play multiple sports is because it improves different muscle sets and keeps certain muscles, ligaments, and joints from being overused. I therefore feel it is a must for the athletic director to get all the coaches to work together and support each other's programs. There are many ways to do this. One way is to have coaches go to other sports' games and take their players with them; the other coaches and kids will notice. Another way is to have a coaches' breakfast, where different coaches speak so that their fellow coaches get to know them better. Athletic directors should make sure that coaches know their boundaries when it comes to encouraging or discouraging kids to play other sports.

It is a good idea to let players develop their muscle sets for other sports during your season so that it won't interfere with the muscle sets necessary for your sport. An example of this is to let kids who play basketball and baseball throw all through the basketball season. If you don't, they will throw anyway in January and February, and then they will mess up their shot just before tournaments. Basketball and football coaches should divide up the spring for players they share so that both sports can have good spring practices.

Some of my best friends are coaches from other sports. Our common bond is the respect we have for each other.

Strategies, Drills, and Offenses

Up three points at the end of a game

Time and again, I have watched coaches whose teams are up three points allow their opponent to shoot a three-pointer at the end of the game. In most cases, they make a crazy shot. Why? Because everyone wants to be a hero. Adrenaline kicks in, and their senses are enhanced; for a short period of time, they are superheroes.

Why are coaches afraid to put the outcome of a game into their own hands? I believe it is because they do not practice fouling in this situation, or they may not trust their players. I have yet to see someone fouled in this situation and that team successfully tie the game. Think about it: First, the player has to make the first shot; then he has to hit the rim and miss the second; then his team has to get the offensive rebound even though you have inside position and more players on the line. If they get the rebound, they must hit the shot. After all of that, they still have only tied the game.

Really, which is easier—a hard three-pointer or the steps just mentioned?

Ask Coach Calipari when Kansas hit a three-pointer to tie the game against Memphis and win the 2008 national championship in overtime. If Calipari had a chance to replay those last few seconds, I bet he would have fouled. I bet he didn't want to foul because he didn't trust his players to carry it out correctly because they hadn't practiced it enough.

Tie games

When the score is tied, and the other team has the ball and is holding it for the last shot, what are your options? There are six possible scenarios:

1. You steal the ball, or they turn it over.

2. They miss, and you get the rebound and play overtime.

3. They miss and get the rebound, score, and win the game.

4. You foul them on the last-second shot, and they make a free throw and win.

5. You foul them on the last-second shot, they miss both free throws, and you play overtime.

6. They make the last-second shot and win the game.

In all of these cases but one, the best outcome you could hope for is overtime. If you let your opponent take the last-second shot, you are allowing their best player to take a prime opportunity to best you. I propose fouling the worst free-throw shooter on the other team immediately. Here are the possible outcomes for this strategy:

1. He misses the front end of a one-and-one, and you have enough time to get a good shot at the other end.

2. He makes the first free throw and misses the second, and you have enough time for a good shot at the other end.

3. He makes two free throws, and you have enough time to score at the other end.

If you decide to foul, it must be practiced; I do not think you should foul if there are less than ten seconds left on the clock.

Delay game

I know it's not in vogue to hold the ball. One should remember that there is no shot clock in high school basketball, and I'm not sure why there is one in college ball; they tell me it makes the game more exciting. Why holding the ball for twenty seconds of the shot clock and running a pick-and-roll every time is more exciting than five people cutting and screening, I do not know. Regardless of your opinion, one must remember that before the shot clock, there were more shots per minute than there are now.

Anyway, since no one runs a good delay game anymore, I suspect that not many teams can defend a good delay game. What is a good delay game? It's one in which you are always a threat to score; it is one with balance, backdoor threats, live dribble options, and hard to trap. In a good delay game, you should be able to take the last shot each quarter.

I used the delay game as an offense to score in the seventies against an aggressive defense. You need more than one set to run against man and zone defenses. (I have included my delay game sets elsewhere in this book.) Without a delay game and because of the three-point shot, a ten-point lead often disappears simply because you are playing to keep from getting beaten.

In a good delay game, you should be able to increase the lead instead of only holding on to win. Sometimes, you can use a delay game when the other team is on a run to slow their momentum. A delay game comes in handy to take time off the clock when you are in foul trouble: If you can take the last shot every quarter, you can get up to three extra shots each game. Remember, the only shots you want are layups and free throws at the end of the game because, if you are running the delay game as an offense, you want high-percentage shots.

Special situations

One way to end or begin a practice is to work on special situations. You should keep a list of special situations and add to it as you see fit. Work on one every day.

Some of the most evident special situations should be worked on at least once per week. Some examples are:

■ The offense is up one point with thirty seconds on the clock.

■ Five seconds are left on the clock at the end of a quarter, and the other team is shooting a one-and-one.

■ You are running inbounds plays with one, three, and five seconds on the clock.

These are only a few scenarios, and you should have a plan for each. Drawing up a new play in the huddle is doomed to fail. Players will get left and right mixed up. Remember: You should run all inbounds plays from the left and right sides.

The art of fouling

If you are behind in the last quarter, you need to extend the game in order to have a chance to come back. The problem is, if you foul the wrong person, he will probably extend the lead. If your best offensive players foul, they will have fouled out at the end.

Whom you should foul should be on your game prep sheet. You should also check the scorebook to see who is missing free throws that night. Another thought is to foul their most cerebral player: This player will probably be more aware of the importance of making or missing the shot, and this might cause him to feel the pressure more.

When should you foul? If you are behind by ten points or

more at any time during the fourth quarter, you should foul a certain player or players at every opportunity. You should let them be open to catch the ball and then aggressively start trying to punch it out. You should have two players from your bench trained to foul without it being flagrant or appearing intentional. It helps if they are a Type A personality and enjoy the role.

The other end of the offense should be inside-out: The ball should be driven in hopes of drawing a foul and, if stopped, it should be kicked out for a three-pointer or another drive. There probably won't be enough time to run through an offensive set. Remember: A bad shot is a turnover.

If the other team runs a four-corner-type offense, double-team the ball when it is not in the middle and force a skip pass; have the top help-side defender playing center field.

Conditioning

Develop a plan of what to accomplish during conditioning. I concentrate on stamina, explosions, quickness, strength, and flexibility.

Stamina is necessary to win the fourth quarter. Most games are decided during the first and last two minutes of each half. Distance running is key—lungs must be expanded to hold more oxygen to send to tired muscles. Distance running should be done monthly during preseason and during breaks in the schedule. Distance running should be done last, or you will not get anything else done in practice.

I try to chart desired times for each player and record their times. I like to start with a half mile and go up a half mile every fourth run until you get to three miles. Then drop a half mile every two runs; then go back up to three. You should run at least three times per week.

For explosions and quickness, drills such as suicides, defensive slides, run and jumps (Celtics), the Marquis Johnson drill, and thirty-second slides work well. The weight room, jumprope, stretching, and hanging are all important for strength and flexibility.

Following are descriptions and diagrams of the drills I mentioned above.

Suicides (line touches)

The first suicide is to the free-throw line and back in three seconds. The second is to the free-throw line and back, and center line and back, in ten seconds. The third is to the free-throw line and back, then center line and back, then the other free-throw line and back, in twenty seconds. For the fourth suicide, repeat the third and add in the end line, increasing the time to thirty seconds. Players must touch every line with their hands. If a line is missed, everyone must do it all over again from the beginning; this teaches players that they are totally dependent on each other to succeed.

Defensive slides

You must stay in your defensive stance and zigzag up and down the gym floor.

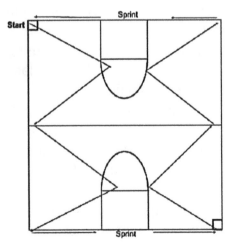

Run and jumps (Celtics)

Players jog from one end to the other. The whistle blows, and players stop jogging and start jumping as high as they can, with their hands up (about ten jumps). The coach blows the whistle again, and players resume jogging. Do this about three or four times as they jog to the other end of the court and back.

Marquis Johnson drill

With two feet together at the end line, on the whistle, the players jump, keeping both feet together. They should count how many jumps it takes them to get to the other end.

High knees

Players should jog from one end of the court to the other, trying to hit their chins with their knees and their butts with their heels.

Rim or backboard touches

Players jump under the backboard as fast as they can, touching either the backboard or rim as many times as they can for thirty seconds.

Thirty-second slides

The player starts in the center of the lane. His partner is his counter. At the whistle, he slides to touch a line with his hand and then touches the other line. There is an imaginary line in the center. Every time, he touches a line or crosses the imaginary line. The goal is forty to fifty touches and crosses total.

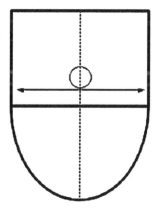

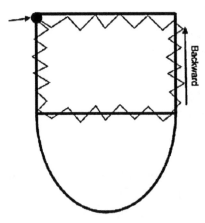

Thirty-second dribbles

The player dribbles from inbounds to the free-throw line, across the free-throw line, backward to the end line, and across to where he began until thirty seconds are up. The goal is to reach ten to twelve repetitions. The player must touch each corner with his hands.

Lunges

This drill is self-explanatory.

Dribbling suicides

These are the same as suicides, but players run this drill while dribbling a ball—with the right hand going up and left hand going back. Adjust the times to fit the ability of the team. Players must touch the line with their hands.

Free throws and sprints

Divide your team into groups of five. Put each group at a different free-throw line. If a player misses, he runs a sprint. If three free throws are made in a row, and a person misses, he runs four sprints. The goal is to make ten free throws in a row. If a group makes ten in a row before the time is up, they do not have to run any more sprints. This could be a five-, eight-, or ten-minute drill.

Things half-court defenses must do to beat good teams

1. Contest the shot.
2. Force catches outside the comfort zone.
3. Defend the high post.
4. Deny the low post.
5. Front all cutters.
6. Jump to the ball.
7. Hold out the arms.
8. Check out.
9. Help and recover.
10. Take charges.
11. Mix deny (red) and sag (green) defenses.
12. Help off the worst players onto the post or best players.
13. Communicate.
14. Go over the top of scoring screens.
15. Step out on screens.

Things full-court defenses must do to beat good teams

1. Pressure structured teams to speed up their tempo.
2. Use a sagging press to slow the tempo vs. teams that run.
3. Play more players if you have a deep bench.
4. Have the correct personnel (long, quick, smart).

Man vs. zone defense

1. Man defense can be adjusted to be almost like a zone.
2. Man gives specific checkout responsibilities.
3. In man defense, you put your best defensive player on their best offensive player.
4. Zone keeps you from having mismatches.
5. Zones stop the screen and roll offenses.
6. Zones are easier to start the fast break out of than man.
7. Zones are good against teams that cannot shoot the three-pointer and teams that do not pass well.

Man drills

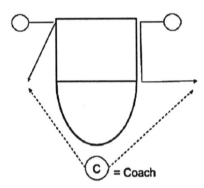

Five minutes—one-on-one
■ Start by denying the pass.
■ The offensive player works on the V cut and L cut.
■ You must contest the shot and check out the shooter.
■ The offensive player works on start-stop dribble, crossover, speed, control, and cutaway.

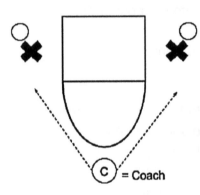

Five minutes—two-on-two
■ Help and recover.
■ Jump to the ball.
■ Take the charge.
■ Weak side and ball side check out.

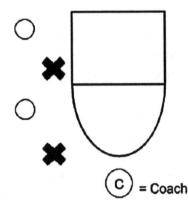

Five minutes—two-on-two ball-side defense
■ Help on the dribble drive.
■ Deny passes.
■ Defend the back door.
■ Check out.

Five minutes—two-on-two help on post

■ Help and recover.
■ Check out.
■ Jump to the ball.

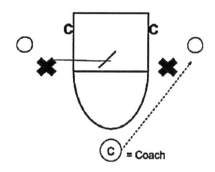

Five minutes—three-on-three guard and cover down

■ The X1 defender intentionally gets beaten on the baseline.
■ X2 helps the side defender jump to the ball and prepares to take the charge.
■ X3 covers down.
■ X1 recovers to O3.

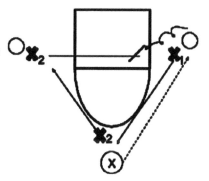

Five minutes—three-on-three defend pass and get through screen

■ Jump to the ball.
■ Go over the top of the screen.

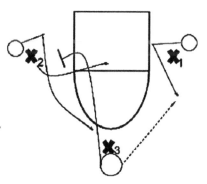

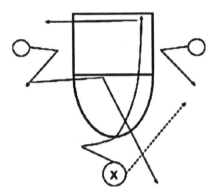

Five minutes—three-on-three jump to the ball and front the cutter

This is great to use in the cutthroat drill.

■ The defenders play with their hands behind their backs.

■ The defense jumps to the ball.

■ The offense passes and cuts down the lane.

■ Never take fakes away from the ball.

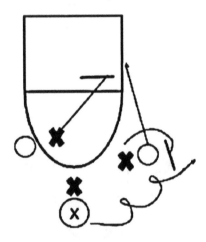

Five minutes—three-on-three ball screens

■ Step out on screens.

■ Go over the top of screens.

■ Help side plays the roll pass.

Five minutes—three-on-three wing screen and roll

■ Step out on the screen.
■ Call the screen.
■ Go over the screen or switch the screen.
■ Go behind the screen.
■ Double-team the screen.
■ Off side is help-side defender.

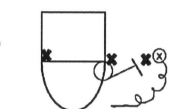

Five to eight minutes—four-on-four shell

■ Jump to the ball.
■ Hands should be behind the back on passes.
■ Contest the shot.
■ Help and recover on the dribble drive.
■ Check out.
■ Transition defense to the other end.

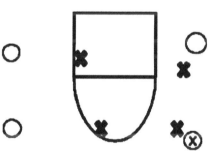

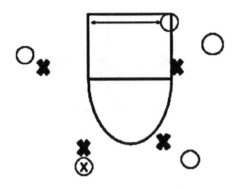

Five minutes—five-on-four shell

■ This is the same as four-on-four shell.

■ Players must help on ball-side post.

■ Stay on defense the entire time (about six trips).

■ Check out on the shot; set the ball down.

■ 1, 2, and 3 backpedal to other end.

■ Offense can work on primary and secondary transition.

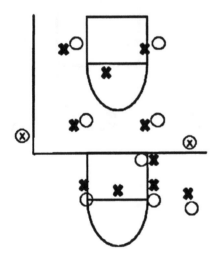

Five minutes—get a five-second count on inbounds

■ Your man doesn't touch the ball.

■ Switch all screens.

■ Take the charge when switching screens.

■ Put a man on the ball at the end line.

■ On the sideline, the man on the ball plays center field and traps the first pass.

One-on-one—on-ball defense rules

■ The hand should be under or touching the ball.

■ Don't come out of your stance.

■ If the ball is in the offensive player's right hand, the defender should have his right hand and right foot up.

■ If the ball is in the offensive player's left hand, the defender should have his left hand and left foot up

■ Never give the offense room to cross over.

■ Do one-on-one drills with hands behind the back.

Red defense rules

■ Four out of five defenders play deny defense.

■ The defender who is farthest from ball is the help defender.

■ The man on the ball must put pressure on the ball (trace the ball).

■ When the dribbler starts to penetrate the lane, all defenders are potential defenders.

■ Check out.

Green defense rules

■ Four out of five are help defenders.

■ The man on the ball plays red defense.

■ Help-side defenders have two feet in the lane.

■ Ball-side defenders have one foot close to the lane and help the post defender.

■ The ball-side post defender always plays red defense.

Post defense drills

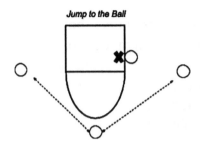

Jump to the Ball

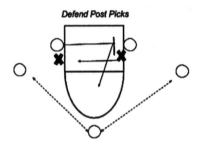

Defend Post Picks

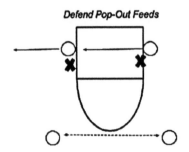

Defend Pop-Out Feeds

Post defense rules

Three ways
1. Deny (front).
2. Side front (free-throw line extended rules).
3. Play behind.

Front
■ If the post is a major threat.
■ If the defender is smaller.
■ If you are in red defense.

Side front
■ If the offense passes well.
■ If the offense plays high-low.
■ To get better checkout position.
■ If the defender is quicker than the offensive player.

Play behind:
■ If the post is not a threat.
■ If they don't use the post as a passer.
■ To get better checkout position.
■ If you are playing in green defense.

Flex offense

- Player 1 passes to player 4 coming off the down pick from player 2.
- Player 3 cuts off the screen from player 5.
- Player 1 down-screens for player 5.
- Player 1 pops out to the corner.
- Run again to the other side.

Why don't you see flex anymore? Answer: Poorly set and used screens.

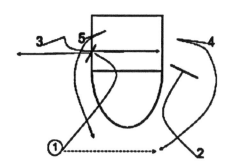

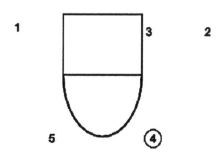

Flex offense corner option

- Player 4 passes to player 2.
- Player 2 feeds the post or passes to player 1.
- Players 4 and 5 both down-screen for player 1.

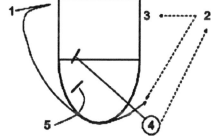

Result:

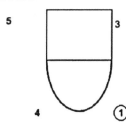

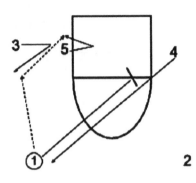

Corner option—replace and feed post
(This is too easy, but it works.)
■ Player 1 passes to player 3.
■ Player 5 fakes a cross screen and quickly replaces himself.
■ Player 1 screens player 4.
■ Player 4 goes to player 1's spot and player 1 goes to player 4's spot.

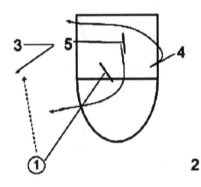

Corner option—cross screen
■ Player 1 passes to player 3.
■ Player 5 screens across for player 4.
■ Player 1 screens player 5.

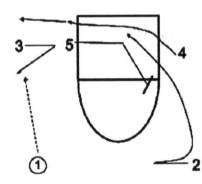

Corner option—back door
■ Player 1 passes to player 3.
■ Player 5 fakes a screen to player 4, then back-screens player 2.
■ Player 4 crosses the lane to clear the lane.

Backdoor vs. overplay

Anytime there is an overplay, players must back-screen instead of down-screen.

Note: Create your own plays to fit your personnel.

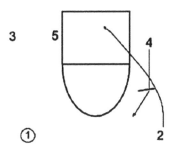

Fist flex

This gives you plenty of room to backdoor.

■ Fist flex follows the same rules as regular flex.

■ Use the free-throw line extended as the baseline.

■ Use chairs in practice across the baseline extended.

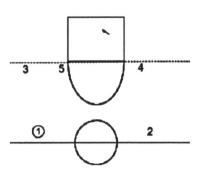

Tight flex set

■ This follows the same rules as above.

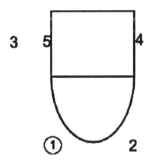

Speed flex

■ Run as fast as possible.

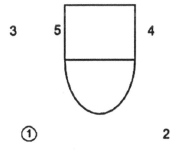

Flex motion rules (four out, one in)

Note: Players must call the name of the player being screened.
1: If the player passes right, the player screens left.
2: If the player passes left, the player screens right.
3: A skip pass is the same as two passes; the player skips screens and gets screened again.
4: The post player can screen anyone, including the ball.
5: The post screener replaces the position screened, and the replaced player becomes the screener.
6: If the ball is passed from the corner, the corner screens the post.

Examples

Rule 1

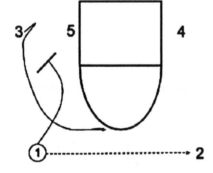

Rule 2

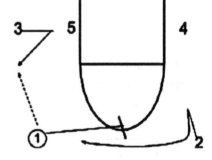

Rule 3

Rules 4 and 5

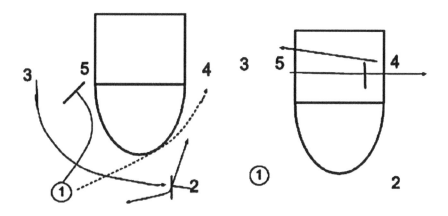

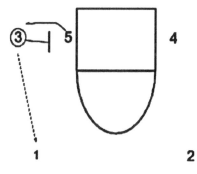

Rule 6

Hybrid guard cross

■ Player 1 passes to player 3.

■ Player 1 cuts off player 5.

■ Player 1 screens player 4, then goes off side corner.

■ Player 2 cuts behind player 1 off of player 5 for a pass from player 3 OR player 2 sets a screen for player 4, then circles back to the original position.

■ Player 3 V-cuts to get open, then receives the pass from player 1.

■ Player 3 passes to player 2 OR dribbles off a screen from player 5, running a pick-and-roll.

■ Player 4 comes off the pick from player 2,

■ Player 4 can flex-cut to the low post OR come off a down pick from player 1 for a high-point shot.

■ Player 5 sets the ball screen for player 3, then rolls to the basket on the shot corner after players 1 and 2 pass by.

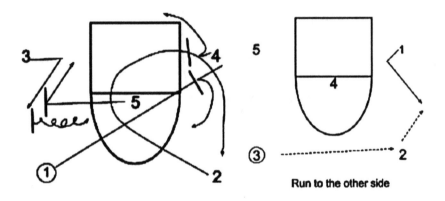

Run to the other side

Triangle offense

This is a simple offense used
when you have two talented
post players and at least two
good three-point shooters.

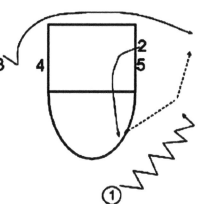

■ Player 1 passes to player 2
or player 3 to feed the post.
■ Players 4 and 5 play a two-
man game screening, cutting,
and high-low.
■ If the post receives the ball
at the high post, they can
high-low feed, drive, or kick out for a three-pointer.

Circle vs. zone (purpose is to get a quick shot)

■ Player 1 passes to player 2 in the corner.
■ Player 2 dribbles up to the wing.
■ Player 1 circles to the same corner for a shot.
■ Player 2 passes to player 1.
■ If player 1 doesn't have a shot, he dribbles to the wing.
■ Player 2 circles to the same corner.
■ As player 1 or player 2 dribbles up, they should be able to
throw a skip pass to player 3.

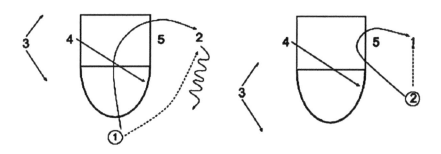

Man load

- Players 2 and 3 either pop out or cross.
- Player 1 passes to player 3 on the high wing (or player 2).
- Player 1 then screens for player 2.
- Player 5 screens for player 4.
- If player 4 doesn't get the ball, player 4 goes to the corner and player 5 comes back to the ball-side post.
- The ball can be reversed to player 2.
- Player 2 passes to player 1.
- Player 4 runs off a screen for player 5 OR player 5 can pop out to the corner.

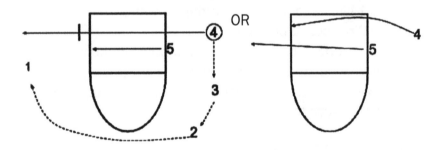

Roscoe (named for Roscoe Williams, former coach at Lambuth College)

■ Player 1 dribbles off player 4's ball screen.
■ Player 2 screens for player 3; player 3 goes to the corner.
■ Player 4 rolls to the rim.
■ Player 5 screens player 2.

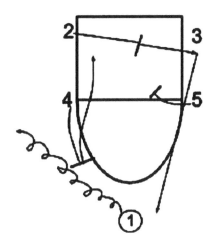

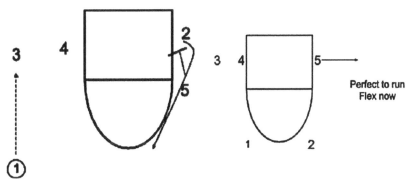

Chaser vs. man on zone

■ Player 3 has the freedom to roam the entire baseline.
■ Players 4 and 5 play a two-man game.
■ You must create options that fit your team.
■ You can swap players 1, 2, and 3 to keep a fresh chaser.

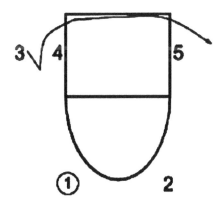

Alley-oop vs. 2-3 or 1-2-2 zone

■ Players must swing the ball from side to side first to get the defense spread.

■ Players 2 and 3 need to be as close to the baseline as possible to get the backline to guard them.

■ As the ball is coming back to player 1 from player 3, player 4 drives into the lane, forcing the middle defender to guard him.

■ Player 5 back-screens the defender on that side.

■ Player 3 slides behind player 5 for the pass.

■ The pass should be aimed at the corner of the backboard.

■ If the pass cannot be made, player 5 should step in front of player 4 in the middle of the lane for a pass.

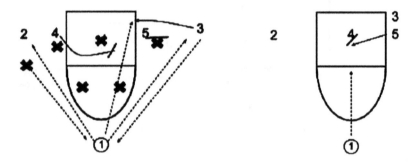

First one delay vs. zone and zone trap

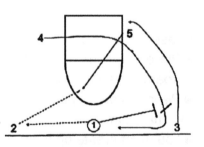

■ Player 1 passes to player 2.

■ Player 2 passes to player 5.

■ Player 4 crosses the lane.

■ Player 4 back-screens player 3.

■ Player 4 replaces player 3.

■ Player 1 screens for player 4.

■ Player 2 or player 5 passes to player 4.

■ Anytime someone is not open, they backdoor, replace themselves, or down-screen.

Zone load

Zone load has the same basic rules as man load with cuts and replacements instead of picks. You can run this offense versus a sagging man-to-man. I created load because a team we played changed defenses every trip down the floor, causing us to read the defense and run the proper offense, confusing us. So we ran load against all of their defenses. It isn't the most exciting offense, but its simplicity and the fact that you overload the sides cause overshifting because you continuously have someone flashing into the high post. This makes guards focus on not overplaying.

- Player 1 passes to player 2 or player 3.
- Player 5 pops to the corner.
- Player 3 passes to player 5.
- Player 4 flashes to the high post or low post.
- Player 2 flashes to the high post and then to the point.
- Player 1 replaces player 2.
- Swing the ball and do the same thing to the other side.
- Always be prepared to skip-pass.
- Use dribble penetration to create open passes.

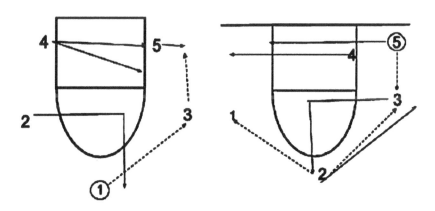

Vanderbilt delay

This offense was created by former Vandy coach Ray Skinner
in the 1950s.

■ Player 1 dribbles off of a screen from player 5. If player 1 is
open, he takes it to the hole.

■ As player 1 is coming off of player 5's screen, player 3
backdoors and then flashes to the top.

■ Player 1 will probably dribble to the right wing and pass to
player 3 up top or to player 5 sliding down to the low block.

■ If player 1 passes to player 3, player 3 will do the same thing
to the other side.

You can add screens or cuts to players 4 and 5.

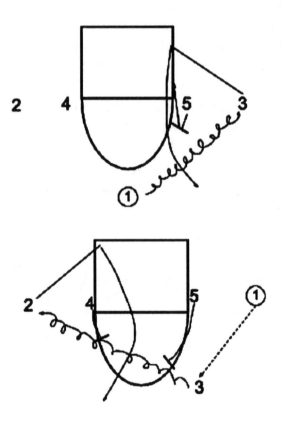

Who do you cut? Who do you keep?

+ Talent + Attitude − Worker **C**	− Talent + Attitude + Worker **B**
+ Talent + Attitude + Worker **D**	+ Talent − Attitude − Worker **A**

■ Coaches have to be judges, so have a plan.

■ Most kids fall into one of these four models.

   ■ There are exceptions because of factors such as ADD, family problems, girl/boy problems, and personalities.

■ Introverts and extroverts have their differences.

   ■ Extroverts are easier to coach unless they are extreme.

   ■ Introverts have to mature into the game. You must appeal to their intellect.

■ When choosing a team, talk to players, teachers, and students whom you know best.

■ Take all who fit Model D and work down from there.

■ I try to keep one kid from Model A. Read "Win-Win" to learn why I do this.

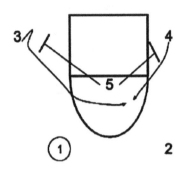

Triple post vs. one-guard front zone

■ Posts can screen each other or run triangle cuts.

■ Posts should pin and seal to create space in the lane.

■ Player 5 screens player 3.

■ Player 3 goes to the high post.

■ Player 3 screens player 4.

■ Player 4 screens player 5.

2-3 offense vs. 1-2-2 or gimmick defense

■ Player 1 passes to player 3 popping out.

■ Player 4 slides down.

■ Player 5 pops up.

■ Player 3 passes back to player 1, and player 3 immediately flashes, pins, and seals.

■ Player 5 slides back to the original spot and pins the back-side defender.

■ Player 1 passes to player 2, and player 4 goes to the ball-side corner.

■ Repeat.

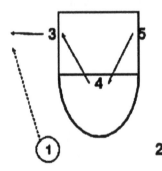
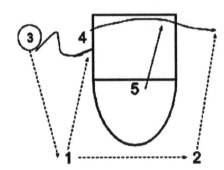

Other shooting drills
1. Partner shooting one, two, and three passes
2. Rapid-fire free throws
3. Rapid-fire shooting
4. One-hand free throws
5. Duke 1-7 shooting progression
6. Three-man shooting
7. Line free throws
8. Double free-throw gotcha
9. Double three-point gotcha
10. Thirty-second shooting
11. Double pick-and-roll
12. Bad screen, good screen

Partner shooting (one pass)

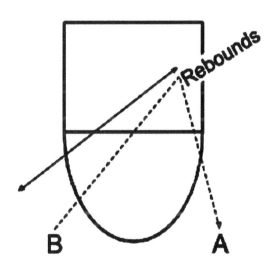

■ Pick a spot for each player to shoot.
■ Remember to take game shots at game spots at game speed.
■ Player B shoots and gets his own rebound, then passes to player A.
■ Player A calls for the ball, shoots, and passes to player B. This is continued for one minute.
■ The goal is to make ten shots. Players must do five push-ups for each shot less than ten.

Partner shooting (two passes)

■ Player A is the only shooter.

■ Player A shoots, rebounds, and passes to player B (player B must call for the ball).

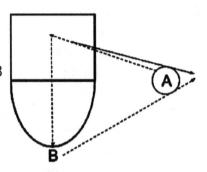

■ Player A then makes an offensive cut, receives the ball from player B, and shoots. This is continued for one minute.

■ The goal is to make ten shots. Players must do five push-ups for each shot less than ten.

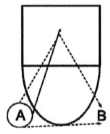

Partner shooting (three passes)

■ This is the same as one-pass shooting but with three passes. Players must call for the ball.

Rapid-fire free throws

■ Players A and C start with the ball in hand.

■ As soon as player A shoots, player C hands him a ball, and he shoots.

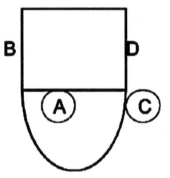

■ Players B and D rebound and pass to player C, who hands to player A.

■ The goal is twelve shots made in one minute.

■ Players must do five push-ups for each shot made less than twelve.

Rapid-fire shooting

■ Pick two close spots to shoot from.
■ Player A runs to spot 1, and player B passes the ball to player A.
■ Player A shoots and runs to spot 2.
■ Player D passes to player A. Player A shoots and runs to spot 1.

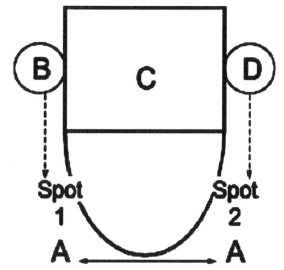

■ This is done for one minute.
■ After one minute, shoot a one-and-one while the players are winded.
■ Rotate positions until everyone has shot.
■ The goal is twelve shots.
■ Players B, C, and D are rebounders.

One-hand free throws

1. Put the ball in your shooting hand with your palm up at your waist.
2. Using only the shooting hand, turn your arm and hand to the shooting pocket.
3. Shoot.
4. Do this ten times. It teaches players to have a balanced shot and follow-through.

Duke (left side) 1-7

Three balls are needed for this drill.

Duke 1

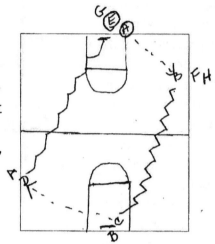

■ Player A passes to player B, and player B shoots a layup.
■ Player C gets either the rebound or made shot. (If the shot was made, the ball must be inbounded).
■ Player C passes to player D, and player D shoots a layup at the other end.
■ As soon as players A and B cross the center line, players E and F do the same as players A and B.
■ Player B gets the rebound and passes to player A. Player A shoots a layup.
■ Players E and F begin when players C and D cross the center line.
■ Players G and H get players C's and D's rebounds and go.

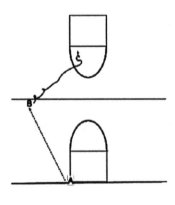

Duke 2

■ Player A passes to player B, and player B shoots a jump-stop jump shot.
■ Everything else is just like Duke 1.

Duke 3
■ Player A passes to player B.
■ Player B dribbles to the free-throw line and passes to player A for a layup.

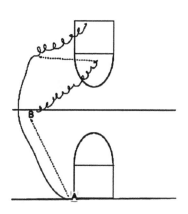

Duke 4
■ Player A passes to player B.
■ Player B dribbles to the free-throw line and passes to player A for a jump shot.

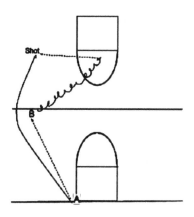

Duke 5
■ Give and go.
■ Player A passes to player B.
■ Player B dribbles to the free-throw line and passes to player A.
■ Player B then cuts to the bucket to wait for a pass from player A.
■ Player B shoots a power layup.

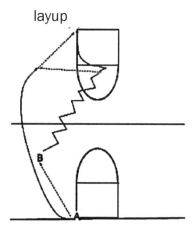

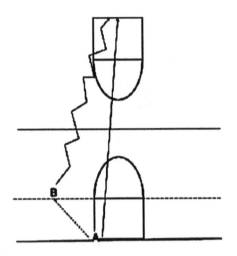

Duke 6—chaser
■ Player A passes to player B and then tries to catch him before he shoots a layup.
■ Player A slaps up at the ball as he goes past player B.

Duke 7—home run and dunk
■ Player A passes to player B around the center line on the fly for a dunk.
■ Always throw to the inside shoulder.
■ Always pronate your wrist on the pass.

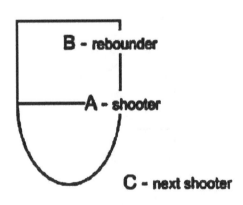

Three-man shooting
■ Player A shoots.
■ Player B gets the rebound and passes to player C but tries to block player C's shot.
■ Player A gets the rebound and passes to player B but tries to block player B's shot.
■ Players should shoot game shots.

Line free throws (for punishment, pressure shooting, or conditioning)

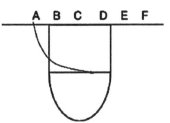

- Have the team line up in two groups on each end.
- Group 1: Player A shoots a one-and-one.
- If he misses the second shot, the group runs one sprint.
- The shooter runs the sprint from the free-throw line. If anyone catches him, they do not have to run the next sprint.

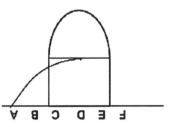

- The shooter has to run his sprints at the end.
- Do the same routine for group 2.
- Run this drill until time is up or a group makes six shots in a row.

Double free-throw gotcha

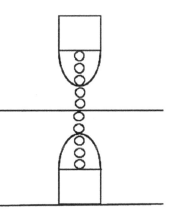

- Play gotcha, but no one gets out.
- If a player gets put out, he gets a point and goes to the other end.
- Players stay in the same line until they get put out.
- When someone gets ten points, the game is over.
- Players run a sprint for each point they have.

Double three-point gotcha

- This has the same rules as free-throw gotcha but is played from the three-point line.

Thirty-second shooting

Two-pointers count as two points. Three-pointers count as three points.

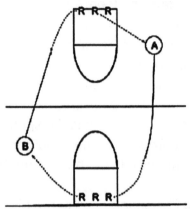

■ Players A and B run from one end to the other, shooting two-pointers and/or three-pointers.
■ Rebounders call the score out loud.
■ The goal is to reach twenty points.
■ R is the rebounder.
■ Rebounders pass to the shooters.

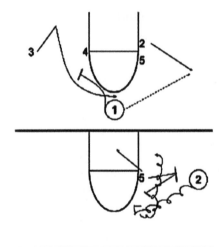

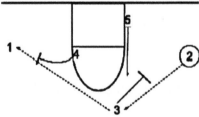

Double pick-and-roll

■ Player 1 passes to player 2.
■ Player 5 screens player 2 with the ball and rolls.

OR

■ Player 5 re-screens the ball and rolls.
■ Player 3 cuts to the top of the key or backdoors.
■ Player 2 passes to player 3.
■ Player 3 passes to player 1, and player 4 sets a screen on player 1, the same as the other side.

Bad screen, good screen (quick hitter for a three-pointer)
- Player 1 has the ball.
- Player 5 pops out to the wing.
- Player 3 goes to the corner.
- Player 5 sets a bad screen for player 3.
- Player 3 leaves a wide gap for the defense to get through.
- Player 5 then sets a good back screen for player 3.
- Player 1 then passes to player 3 for a shot.
- Player 1 screens for player 2.
- Player 4 flashes to the low post.

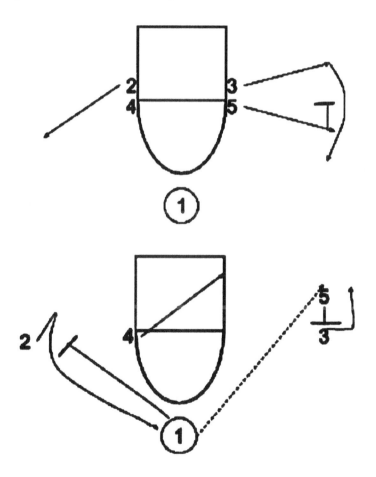

Three-on-three full-court cutthroat

I start this drill in half-court cutthroat and then turn it into full-court.

■ If team 1 scores, team 2 is off.

■ Team 1 transitions to the other end against team 4.

■ If team 2 gets the rebound, they will scrimmage until one of the teams scores.

■ The team that scores transitions to the other end, and the other team is off.

Example:

■ The 1s miss, and the 2s get the rebound and go to the other end as the 1s transition into defense.

■ The 2s miss, and the 1s get the rebound and go to the other end.

■ The 1s score and transition to the other end. They are guarded by the 4s.

■ The 1s miss, and the 4s get the rebound and score. The 4s go to the other end and are guarded by the 5s.

■ The 4s score and transition to the other end. They are guarded by the 3s.

You can change it up. When the defense gets the ball, the offense goes off.

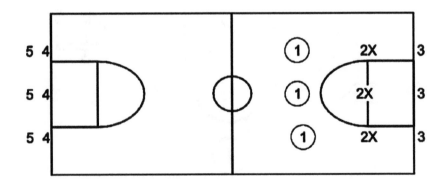

Three-team scrimmage

If you are going to play a team that does not press and do a good job getting back on defense or run changing defenses, especially half-court traps, this is a good drill. It is a good way to teach your team how to recognize defenses.

■ You need fifteen players and a coach on each end calling defenses.

■ If a team scores, they stay on the offense. They inbound and go to the other end.

■ The point guard must call the offense.

■ Coaches on each end will call the defense while the ball is on the other end.

Options:

1. You can designate a certain player to be the only shooter.
2. You can run your last-second shot plays.
3. You can run your delay game.
4. You can run your quick hitters.

And so on . . .

Wolfpack last-second shot

In 1983, Jim Valvano's North Carolina State Wolfpack won the NCAA national championship on a short shot that was caught and put in at the buzzer. Why did this happen? First, the defense was busy checking out, and they were not trained to rebound an air ball. Second, the offense was watching the ball more than the defense.

So why not shoot the ball from the wing, aiming in front of the rim? Have a post-to-post screen and a post, go for the rim to catch, and put in the air ball.

Some scenarios:

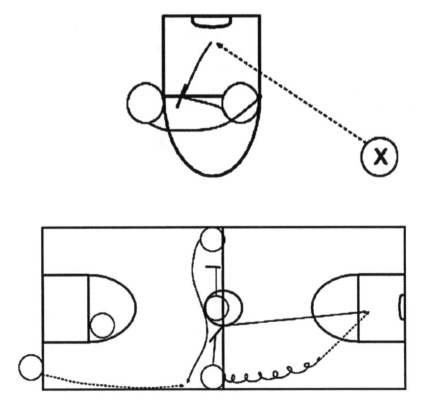

Conclusion

The orchard

When my daddy was sixty-two years old, he called and asked me if I would come over one Saturday morning to help him plant an orchard. Daddy never abused the use of his kids, so I figured he really needed my help. I have never said no to my daddy, and I was happy to spend a day with him.

When I got there at about eight o'clock in the morning, I had no idea that we were going to plant more than a hundred small peach and apple trees by hand. It was hard work, and I was not used to it. By the time we got about halfway through, I told Daddy that it would be at least ten years before any of the trees would be able to produce fruit. I asked him why he was doing all this work with such little benefit. His answer was simple: "Somebody will."

My daddy didn't live to die; he lived to live. Life wasn't about only him; it was about getting the most out of life each and every day. Well, we got the trees planted. My mamma made us a great lunch, and I didn't go home until the sun went down. The next spring, my daddy had a heart attack and died. At the funeral, my thoughts went to that day, planting the orchard. I hope I can live life to its fullest until I die, too.

Because of my health, I had to retire from the job I had loved for more than forty years. For two years, I had a hard time adjusting to retirement. I even substitute-taught just to be around kids. Finally, though, my thoughts went back to the orchard. My grandson mentioned us starting a record store. I knew nothing about starting a business, but then again, my daddy didn't have any experience raising fruit trees. I now have something new to challenge me, and it is wonderful.

When Pablo Casals reached the age of ninety-five, a young reporter asked him, "Mr. Casals, you are ninety-five and the greatest cellist that ever lived. Why do you still practice six hours a day?"

Casals answered, "Because I think I'm making progress." I think Mr. Casals would have liked my daddy.

Filling the void

I cannot speak for everyone, but there is a void or vacuum inside of me. There are many ways to fill this void, some good and some bad, some temporary and some permanent. Life is a search for the right way to fill the void. Some people use parties, alcohol, drugs, sex, work, or power. Some people try to fill the void by giving to others, education, rationalization, public service, and so on.

I have intentionally and unintentionally tried many of the fillers listed above. Some worked for a little while, and others lasted longer, but two things have become permanent for me: The first is giving my life to my Savior, and the second is finding my earthly soul mate.

The first time I met my future wife, I knew there was

something special about her. Years later, I was blessed to have her become my wife. Nancy is my rock. She is my confidant, my sounding board, my partner, my balancer, and my best friend. She makes me feel smarter and better than I really am. She keeps me grounded and stops me from being reactive. She is my great encourager.

I would never have had the courage to write this book without her. She is more than special. She is part of me.

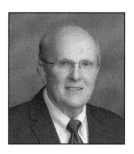

About the Author

Coach Joe North dedicated more than forty years to teaching and coaching basketball at the high school and middle school levels. He compiled an overall record of 853–239 at high schools at Bells, Bolivar, Crockett County, Adamsville, Dyersburg, North Side, and Trinity Christian Academy. He coached middle schools at Michie, Adamsville, and University School of Jackson. He also taught US and world history.

In an interview with News/Talk 101.5 when he was inducted into the Jackson Madison County Sports Hall of Fame in 2019, Coach North explained that he moved to various schools because he was "always looking for a new challenge." Changing schools also showed him that "my coaching style and discipline is transferable to all kids and schools."

Coach North attended Ramer High School in McNairy County, Tennessee, graduating in 1969. He graduated from Lambuth College in 1974 and earned his master's degree from Memphis State University in 1982. He married his wife, Nancy, in 1982, and they have two daughters, Stephanie Cross and Shannon Schuler. His grandson is Hunter Cross, who has two bands, Skeleton Krew and the Hunter Cross Band. Today, Coach North devotes himself to helping his grandson with his music and with his record shop in downtown Jackson.

Coach North welcomes your comments and discussion. Email him at hollowcoach@gmail.com.

CPSIA information can be obtained
at www.ICGtesting.com
Printed in the USA
FSHW021608091221
86663FS